Swing Trading Options

A beginner's guide to start making money online gaining big profits day by day with secret strategies, plots, data analysis and mastering financial leverage and risk management

Douglas Elder

Table of content

Introduction

First, we perhaps need to get familiar with the term options trading. When we talk of options, we are simply talking about the most all-round trading instrument ever found. It can be applied to lower the risk of the expected investments. Options can also be used as a cover over the dwindling stock market to reduce the losses downside.

However, much of these Trading options are very well paying, and you need to know that any trader should at all cost be able to come to an understanding of the risks they exhibit. Therefore, they aren't worth or readily user-friendly to all. When you understand the way options are run or work, and perhaps how to use them, it can call for you as a trader to also understand how the market works well and, as a such, make you a prominent trader and most successful.

Terms to Understand

Derivative

It is of great value to define some terminologies used and will be encountered during this study. An option, therefore, originates from a collection of securities, i.e., it is a fundamental example of these securities.

Therefore a derivative we can simply call it security that has its price entirely dependent on or rather resulting from another asset's price. An immediate layman example we can say that sugar is a derivative of sugarcane. Similarly, all financial securities that have their values tied entirely to the prices of other assets are called derivatives.

An option

An option, in this case, falls under derivatives categorically. The price of an option essentially is connected to the price of another thing. We can as well say that options are simply financial contracts which accord the option buyer the right and not the obligation to either buy or even sell the asset in question at any given current price be it on or even before a given date in the future. We refer the right to sell as a put option whereas the right to buy the existing security as a call option.

In options trading, you will come across several trading terminologies that must be defined to make the whole concept understandable. They are but not limited to, the following:

Short

An option is said to be short as long as it has been sold.

Long

The opposite of short is true in this case. Here the option is already bought and is being held or owned.

Premium

When you hear of premium, it simply refers to the price related to an option contract. It is simply the total amount that one pays to get the option contract, or rather the proceeds that one gets out of the contract is sold.

Call Option

This in brief mandates the buyer the right of buying given security, e.g., stock, at any given fixed price ever referred to as strike price on or even before a given date usually called the expiry date. Similarly, the one selling the call is hence obligated to go ahead and give out the said stock at the strike price as long as the option is exercised.

Put Option

Input option as opposed to call option, the buyer has the right of selling a security at a given fixed price, either on or before the allocated date ever called expiration date.

More so the seller also of the same put is hence obligated with purchasing the stock at the fixed or strike price only if exercised.

Expiry Date

This is the dateline upon which the execution of an option may be carried out.

Strike Price

Ever referred to as exercise price. It's the price that has been set for the buyer or the seller to transact on the allocated asset or underlying asset for that matter.

Assignment and Exercise

Exercise is a procedure whereby buyers of options may invoke the option terms.

Ask

This is the lowermost price which the seller is offering for an option.

Bid

The bid is the uppermost price which a buyer wishes to give out for the specific option.

Volume

This is the overall cumulative number of a specific contract which has traded on the very specific day.

An Option Chain

Before we look at an option chain, let's define an open interest: This is all the number of contracts in the whole world. This number is not constant. That's to say that it is frequently being updated basing on the last day's trade activities.

ITM

This is an acronym that simply abbreviates 'in the money '; these are options that do have an inherent value. It could be called that have strikes beneath or puts that have strikes above with the underlying currently trading.

OTM

It simply signifies the 'out of the money,' which are options with no inherent value. It could be called that have strikes above or puts that have strikes lower with the underlying currently trading.

ATM

'At the money,' these are options which have strike prices nearer the underlying that currently is trading.

Intrinsic Values

We also need to know something concerning the intrinsic value. This is the variation between the strike price and the stock price. The time value on the other side is the potential that an option could embrace higher intrinsic value at a time to come.

Difference Between Options and Stocks

Options are securities that bind you to an agreement. They work almost the same way as stock and futures contracts. However, in options trading, you are not obligated to buy or sell anything as long as you stick to the rules of the agreement. In order to invest better, however, you must understand what makes options different from ordinary stock trading.

Chapter 1: Swing Trading Options

As seen before, an option is a derivative by definition. It is derived from an underlying asset. Stock, on the other hand, is just a financial instrument that indicates ownership of an asset. This means that stock gives you some ownership of an investment or business, but an option does not. Let us look at other differences between the two:

1. An option expires while stock does not. You can hold onto the stocks of a business or company for years without expiring. However, options only exist during the trading period of a particular asset and cease to exist as soon as this period expires. The expiration date for most options is nine months or less although there are longer-term options contracts that can span a period of three years. These are known as LEAPS or long term equity anticipated securities. If an option is not exercised before the expiration date, any premiums put in it may get lost.

2. The fact that you own an option does not give you a share in the underlying security. This is because options are all about giving you the rights to buy

and sell a security; they do not give you any ownership rights.

3. Options carry less influence than stocks. Owning stock means that part of a company belongs to you, and this means that you can influence the direction of the company and also receive dividends from the stock. Owning options, on the other hand, gives you zero rights to the companies involved.

4. Stocks are only profitable when their prices go up, but you can gain profit from options when the prices change both ways. This is made possible by the put and call options discussed above. These enable you to make a profit, whether the prices are increasing or decreasing.

Stock Exchange

Stock exchanges are secondary markets where people who own shares can transact them with potential buyers. It is essential to understand that the corporations in the stock markets do not buy shares or sell them regularly; however, they can engage in share callback or issue of new shares but not on daily operation. Thus when one buys shares from a stock market, they are not buying it from the company but rather from the existing shareholders, correspondingly when one sells their shares they do not sell them to the company but to the potential investors.

Sometimes changes in corporate essentiality require several days, weeks, or even months to cause sufficient price change or swing for one to be able to make a reasonable profit. When this happens, the traders will be holding on their assets, either security mostly stocks or funds waiting for the prices to go high before selling them which amounts to swing trade and making them swing traders.

Swing Trading

Swing trading is a contemplative trading approach in financial markets, where an asset to be transposed is held for several days to a couple of weeks by the trader before selling it to make a profit when the price changes or swings. Swing trade is usually speculative in nature in that a trader waits until the prices go higher before disposing his assets and goes down before buying the assets. Some traders may take trades up to a few months but still, consider it as a swing trade as long as it does not go beyond a trading session.

Mostly, people confuse day trading and swing trading. A day trader holds a stock anywhere starting from a few seconds to hours but never more than a day, while a swing trader examines the vital period and the profits of the sale and keeps the stocks for more than a day but not going beyond the trading session. The difference is the time frame. Most swing traders invest less than the day traders for time as time goes on prices change and the prices can change upward or downward anytime causing massive loses or profits, thus the swing traders portfolio is less than that of a day trader to cub any risk that may arise in case of the unfavorable prices during the downward trend.

Options

This is a derivative financial instrument derived from stocks, equities like indices. An option gives the buyer an OPTION to buy or sell the underlying stock at the set price. The seller of the option must go along with if the buyer has exercised his option.

Options can be categorized in two namely: The calls and The puts

The Calls

This a contract that permits an option buyer to buy an underlying asset at a specific price in a specified period of time frames.

A trader buys an option if he is expecting the price of the underlying asset to go high within a certain time.

The Put

This is the right of the trader to sell an option without being obligated to it.

Traders buy put options if they are anticipating the fall in prices of the underlying asset.

Goals of Swing Trading

The core objective of swing trading is to make profits in a short period of time. For instance, a swing trader buying stocks and waiting for about three days for the price to go high then sell them to the potential buyer is not in this trade for any other thing rather than make more profits in a short period. Limiting risk exposure is a goal that every swing trader must observe when plunging into this trader. As much as swing trading earns you profits in a short period,

it is very risky. It is good that a swing trader must know the risks and the probability precept so as to limit the losses in case the prices go down.

Identification of high probability set up will help a swing trader know when to invest and how much to invest. A swing trader must always be cautious of the trends of the markets; if the market is showing any sign of no gains, one should hold the stocks and sell them at the right time. The trader should be able to identify the patterns, trend directions, and see the short potential of short term changes in trends for the purchase and sale of the assets.

Consistency should be in the mind of every swing trader. One should always be consistent in this trade if you want to remain in the business for long. If you are a buyer, you should be consistent for you to get more customers and more profits in the trade.

Swing traders go in this trade so as to preserve capital. The capital invested in the purchase of securities, especially stock remains in use in this trade without pulling it out to do other things hence earning the capital gains.

Apart from the goals above, at least every swing trader has their other own goals as to why they go into this business. You might be surprised to find out that others are into it for exploration purposes, globalization and political interests, and so on, so goals are never limited to oneself.

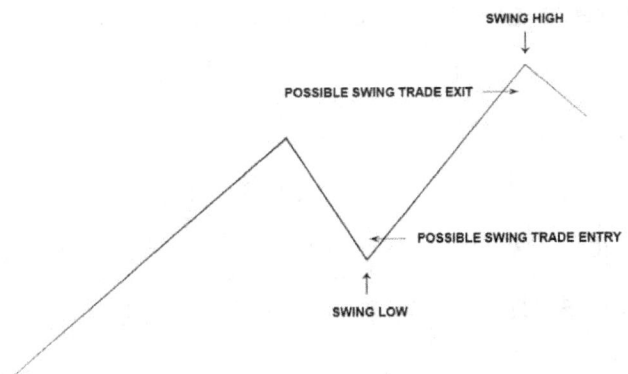

Swing Trading Premiums

A premium is an amount an option seller receives from the option buyer for granting the specified rights in the specified period in the option. This money is paid upfront, and it is not refundable irrespective of the option being exercised or not. Here there is no stock ownership, so no collection of the dividends.

Tactics for Selecting Stocks for Option Premium in Swing Trading

- Make sure to trade the stocks that have strong technical set up for reversal in the price trends. Look at the term patterns; are they going up or down? Is the stock being accepted in the market or rejected? Is there an improvement in the stock in the market?

13

- Trade the known stocks. This will help you get more clients for your stocks. No one is going to run after a stock that is not known because of the risk too high.
- Look back at your trading performance and know which stocks to select. You don't want to put up stocks that just sold highly lately and leave the most stable ones.
- Put up the stocks that are highly discussed in the message boards.

Making a Swing Trade Option Premium Trade

- Make sure you limit your investment. Here, in case of a loss, you can only lose your premium amount, but you are not forced to buy any stock.
- Always buy to open and sell to close the trade of both calls and puts. This will help you avoid buying or selling underlying stocks.
- Make sure you have selected an expiration period that is close but at least beyond the date of purchase that will give you enough time to make a profit from the underlying stock or to get expected reversal in price. There are other long term strategies, but since swing trade is a short

term trader, it is advisable to go for the short time one.

- Make sure you select a strike price that is within 3 to 6 strikes of the total amount.
- Make sure you assess your market well before buying or selling your stocks so as to avoid massive losses or to avoid the stock flood. If you have understood well the environment that is the type of the market you are in, then it will be safer for you to trade. If you want to purchase a call, go for the bullish trend.
- Make sure you have picked an accommodating strike price. Actually what you need is an out of money option but which is not so away and goes into the money.
- Manage your trade. If you feel the instability zooming in, you can lay low and roll your options to the following month where you can put them up for a better price.
- Options for swing trade needs a lot of patience, and therefore one is recommended to go for the purchase of the pullbacks. You can be patient and wait for you to later on trade at a profit. Thus you have to understand when to trade and wait. These are your entries and exits.

How The Premium Works.

The investor buys both an out-of-money call and put option simultaneously, the call option strike price is higher than the current market price while the put option strike is lower than the market price, here there is profit potential for the call option has unlimited if the asset rises in price while the put asset can still profit if the price falls.

The investor here sells an out of money call, and an out of the money put simultaneously. This is neutral, making it earn profit anyway. The profits here are realized if the price of the stock trades narrows the range to breakeven point.

Strategies of Swing Trading Option

Swing trading options requires a bigger time frame and not an intra-day time frame.

I have summed up a few swing trading options strategies that can help you go into the trade and operate it well from start to the end.

There are so many strategies, but we can simply group them into two groups namely:

- Direction strategies

- Non-directional strategies

Direction Option Strategies

We have the flat out calls or puts and the spreads. Here one has to look keenly and analyze the direction of the underlying carefully. Buying a call here only suggests that you are expecting the underlying asset price to increase while buying a put only suggests that you are expecting the underlying price of the asset to go down.

Alternatively, if a trader sells a call, he expects the prices to decline so that he can collect a premium. This strategy is strongly advised against for the risks are too high. This is the same for selling a put; the trader expects the stocks prices to increase so that he can collect a premium. The risk is still high, and it goes as far as $0 for this the furthest stocks can fall to.

Combination Plays

- **The Debit Spreads**

Debit spreads minimize the premium costs but limits the potential gains. Debit spreads works in that one buys an option and sells the same option. Here a trader buys a call by targeting the rise in price but minimizes the premium by selling the same call at a higher amount than the buying price. The premium collected from the higher call offsets the premium collected from the lower call. This is what we call the bull call debit spread. This applies the same to the put debit spread, which is mostly known as the bear put spread. The trader buys an in the money or at the money put and then minimizes the premium paid while selling the out of the money put.

- **Non-Direction Option Strategies**

This includes a combination of calls and puts but in a different way. The credit spread is the most known type of non-direction strategy. It is commonly used in slow markets like especially the summer markets. There are two types of credit spreads namely:

- The bull put spread
- The bear call spread.

The Bull Put Credit Spread

This is where a trader buys a put at a lower strike for fewer premiums than the short put while he sells the put option for a set premium. This brings in net profits and caps risks, unlike selling the puts that are fully exposed to the risks. The risk's capped difference is in the strikes less the premium.

The Bear Call Credit

Spreads It always involves two call options:

- To sell a call to get premium
- To buy a call at a higher strike to get a net credit premium.

In this spread, is capped for it is in the bull put. When the two spreads, the bull put and the bear call spreads are put together, they form a non-directional options combo called the iron condo.

The Iron Condo

This involves the bull put and the bear call coming together and putting the price in between. The goodness with this iron condo is that you cannot lose everything at once.

Volatility Combination

This is a non-directional strategy including the strangles and the saddles which tries to take advantage of instability, which leads up to the earning reports. When the stocks are not stable, usually, which is always the case; they lead up to their earnings reports due to the uncertainty.

The Strangles

Here the investor holds the position of both a call and a put option with different strikes but with the same expiry date of the underlying asset. Strangle is a good strategy, especially if you are unsure of the direction of the underlying asset, but you think that it will increase in price in the near future. Summarily, strangle involves a long put and a long call at two different strikes.

The Straddles

The investor here holds the position of the call and the put option with the same strikes with the same expiry date of the underlying asset. The saddle simply involves the long put and the long call with the same strikes.

The resulting factor of the combination of the strangles and the saddles is that the premiums would increase on the call and put side as the volatility increases. However, if the stocks rise or fall, one side will offset the losses of the other.

Fibonacci Retracement

This a pattern that helps traders be able to understand the strengths of the markets, how to invest in the trade, the dos and the don'ts for them to make profits and also the weakness of the trade that they should be cautious of and look for the possible solutions to so as to be able to earn the profits despite the weaknesses in the trade. They must be able to identify the supporting and resistance levels on the chart. Most of the time, stocks go down to a certain percentage before they bounce off to the previous one.

The Fibonacci are 23.6%, 38.2% and 61.8% on a stock chart. This can help one understand, or they can reveal the reversal. However, most traders also look at the 50% reversal level, although it is not the Fibonacci pattern. A stock swing trader can go into business if the prices that we're facing a downward trend retraces and goes up to the 61.8% retracement level with an expectation of making a sale with a profit when the price goes down and then moves up to 23.6%, Fibonacci line.

Chart: Fibonacci Retracement

Channel Trading

Be able to understand and point out or select high and low tending levels. Make sure you look at the ascending channel, the descending channel and the horizontal channel. If anytime you connect the ascending and the descending channel and get the horizontal channel, then a channel is formed. Channel trading is good for short term trends but not longtime. You simply connect the two low trends and then the higher trends to get a channel.

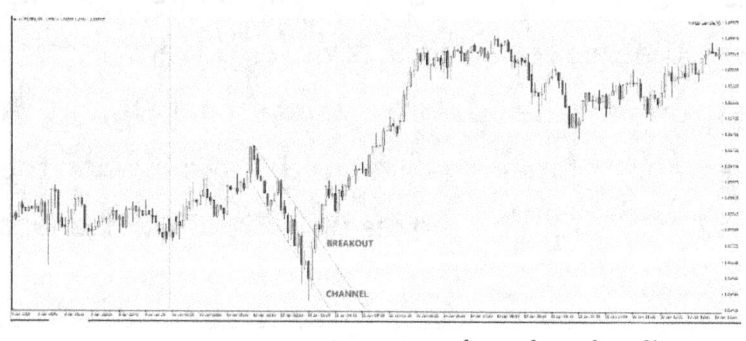

Chart: Channel Trading

10 AND 20-DAY SMA SMAs

Simple Moving Averages

It is also called an arithmetic moving average. It is calculated when you take the closing sums of every calculation then you divide it by the number of time of the periods in the calculation.

The formula for SMAs

A1+A2+...An/n

Where, A = the period of the asset period n

n= the number of total periods.

The SMAs helps one be able to view the price movements and decide when to invest. If the averages point upwards, this only means the prices of the securities are increasing, but if they point downward, this means the prices are decreasing. Short term time frame is more volatile than the longer time frames. Actually, the long time frames are smoother through the shorter ones are close to the data.

The trading patterns that use the SMAs are:

- the Death cross
- the Golden cross

Death cross

This occurs when the 50-day SMA crosses the 200-day SMA. This is like a bearing that is signaling out, showing that more losses are going to be incurred.

Golden cross

It only arises when a long time moving average is above a short time moving average during the breaking of the short term moving average.

MACD Cross Over (Moving Average Convergence Divergence)

It consists of two moving lines. The MACD line and the signal line. This line moves together, but the MACD line happens to move faster than the signal line. The signal line acts as a moving average of the MACD line. A signal line occurs when a MACD line and an average line cross each other. Most of the security traders focus on the movement of these lines to know the momentum.

The traders prefer the signal cross over than the zero cross over. When the signal line is on top of the crossing MACD line, a sale occurs, but when. If a MACD crosses a zero signal from below, this means there is an upward trend, but if it crosses from below, there is a new emergence from the downward trend. When the MACD is above zero, it only means there is an upward trend. When the prices are going high, and the MACD is not, there is divergence. Divergence warns if the price has slowed, but it can never reverse the prices.

The formula of MACD

MACD histogram=MACD Line –Signal Line

EMA means Exponential Moving Average

MACD line= 12 day EMA-26 day EMA

Signal Line=9 day EMA of the MACD Line

Despite this MACD working, it is more of an indicator than a strategy. A much as this indicator works, it is not perfect. It is prone to irregularities like a false signal. It is just an indicator and not a strategy. The MACD does not come with the risk controller making it unable to control costs and profits. The traders, while using this indicator, need to come with the profit and risk management way.

Emphasizing on SMAs and EMA. Most people confuse this two though they are not the same. Their similarity is in their final work of interpretation of fluctuation of prices to the traders, but their differences are that the Exponential Moving Average tries to assign a higher weight to the recent prices and on the other hand the Simple Moving Average gives the same weight to the all the values.

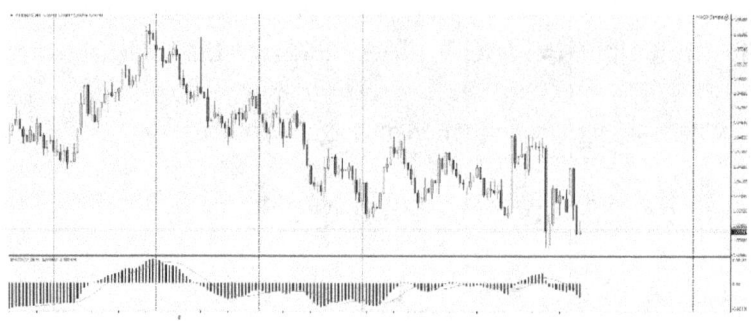

Chart: MACD

Advantages of Swing Trading

- **Exposure To Other Trading Opportunities**

There are several investment opportunities that swing traders indulge in to earn more profits. A trader who plunges in swing trader has this opportunity of investing in single stocks, group of stocks; they can even apply the swing strategies to go into cryptocurrency like bitcoin trade if they want to.

- **Straight forward**

Swing trade is one among the straight forward propositions. It tends to remove the small stocks from the equation, and traders should really go for this. The trade offers to trade with the large-cap stocks, which helps in volatility and volume needed for this swing trade opportunities.

- **More Trading Platforms**

A swing trader is able to operate with different swing trade platforms. Thus he is able to learn more of which platform and trend are more stable for him to invest in. The platforms could be Meta trader, mobile Apps, trader trips, and so on.

- **More Time**

Compared to intraday where a trader has to make decisions and invest immediately, swing trade gives a trader time to be able to choose well as per the convenience time when to invest and how much he wants to invest and also the trader can decide to hold and invest at the time he thinks is more appropriate.

- **Flexibility**

A swing trader is able to move from dealing with single stocks to a group of stocks with much ease.

- **Quick Profits**

It is my assumption that everyone likes money. Swing trading when keenly done earns you money faster than the long-term trading

- **No Need For Daily Monitoring**

Unlike in intraday where a trader has to monitor the price trend every single minute, in swing trade, the trader has quality time before he checks the trends which actually gives him time to attend to other issues.

- **No complicated tools needed**

Swing trading does not need complicated tools and algorithms because this trade is not interested in speed; rather, its interest is in the correct analysis of stock trends or index. Whereas the intraday trade requires sophisticated tools to be able to calcite the quickness and the price changes.

- **Limitation Of Losses**

Since the trader looks at the price trends before buying or selling, one is more likely to know the downward price trend and avoid investing to avoid the loses.

- **Predictability**

In swing trade, there is predictability of the downward trend or upward trend of the prices before investing or putting up a sell of the underlying asset. For instance, the MACD crossover indicator helps swing traders to know when a good time to invest is, and when is the time to hold.

- **Maximization Of Capital**

A trader in swing trade is able to use his capital to the maximum without withdrawing it and investing it elsewhere. This happens mostly during the holding period of the underlying asset awaiting for the prices to go up.

- **Lively**

The securities market is a very lively market. Which trader would want to go to a dormant trade? A swing trader is able to plunge into this market and remain in business for a long time because the trade is always active. If the trade is active, this means there is money moving in and out and profits being made.

- **Losses Are Smaller**

Swing trade being a short term trade, losses are smaller, unlike in long term trade. This helps you invest more in short term trade for the losses are minimized to like 95 to 100 pips, unlike in the long term where the losses could run up to 400 pips.

- **Taking Advantage Of The Natural Ebb And Flow Of Markets**

Since there is a lot of strategies in the swing trade including the indicators like the MACD cross over that predict the trends of the trade, traders tend to take advantage of this flow of the markets to make their profits.

- **Freedom of choice**

In swing trade, a trader has the freedom to choose the type of channel to trade with without being restricted to certain channels only. One is able to choose from ascending channel, descending channel, or horizontal channel. In channel trading, the trader simply looks at the past, and the present compares the two and decides on which channel he wants to choose.

Disadvantages of Swing Trading

- **Subjection to double loss**

When the market shows support or resistance level at a certain area, this does not mean it will remain like this for a long time, it is likely to change, and you can incur losses from time to time.

Chart: Support and Resistance

- **Needs technical analysis knowledge**

Reading the chart if the trends are going upward or downward is not a big issue almost anyone can do that, but understanding your entries and exit points on the chart need a lot of technical analysis knowledge.

- **No capital rotation**

In swing trade, a swing trader locks his money in stocks and is not able to rotate it where he can either gain or lose it all compared to intraday where a trader into capital more often.

- **Assumption**

A swing trader mostly assumes that the prices will go high if the trend has been an upward one and especially if he is using the channel trading which might only end up making him invest more and incur massive losses. Summarily, swing trading options is the trading of the asset securities being held awaiting the sell, where these options are the calls and the puts. Swing trading options strategies can be used by day traders and any other traders to help you run your trade well.

Chapter 2: Factors Influencing Option Prices

Options can ever be priced until one knows what makes up their value. An Options trade is a complex trade that requires a lot of adjustments and analysis in that if you don't know the fundamentals, then you cannot finalize anything. In the option chain, option prices are not just created at random; they are calculated by using the Black-Scholes option-pricing model.

The Black-Scholes Model

This model was coined by Fisher Black and Myron Scholes who came up with a formula that can help theoretical calcite price for financial instruments of with a known expiration date. This model uses variables to calculate the probability that an option will be exercised or will be in- the -money (ITM) at expiration. Originally the Black-Scholes model required five inputs, underlying price or the stoke price, strike price or exercise price, time of expiration, risk-free rate, and volatility, but recently dividends have been added as an input.

The factors include:

Time to Expiration

When an investor exercises the option for a longer period, there are greater chances for it to be in-the-money at the time expiration period. Options lifespan is limited. When an Option has a long time before expiration, its value increases, but if an option has less time to its expiration, its value decreases because it doesn't have enough time to go around in the market.

Volatility

When an underlying asset has high volatility, it is more likely to end in-the-money during the expiration period. Volatility cannot be observed directly because it is impossible, so it can only be estimated or implied. The volatility used here is the forward volatility. The forward volatility is the result of the measure of implied volatility after a specified period in the future.

The implied volatility now shows the movement in the stock's future volatility. It helps tell the thinking of traders about the stock price movements.

The higher the implied volatility, the more people think the stock prices are going to move. Implied volatility is expressed in percentage form, and it is done annually.

Value stocks have lower implied volatility unlike the growth stocks or small caps which have high implied volatility because small caps move around a lot, unlike value stocks which do not move much.

Interest rates

When the interest rates are high, the call option goes high too, while the Put Option goes down. However, interest rates have very little effect on the options. When interest rises, the call options are a good investment, and when it drops the put option is the best. The rise in interest of the call option makes the call option in-the-money while the put option out-the-money and a decrease in the interest, a call option is and out-the-money and a put option is in-the-money.

Stock prices/Underlying prices

The marketable options have different valuation than non-marketable options. For instance, if a call option allows a buyer to buy a stock at a specified price, which is lower than that of the future price, then the option is more worthy.

For example:

An option call allows an investor to buy The Option Prophet (TOP) for $200 while it is trading at $150

An option call allowing a buyer to purchase a TOP at 150 when it is trading at $100

The first one will have a lower value for no buyer is going to purchase an option at a higher price than the trading period.

Most of the buyers will go for the second choice for it is more appealing. Buying an option at a lower price than the trading price whereby the value will be high.

Strike prices/Exercising price

Strike prices are categorized differently as in-the-money, at-the-money, or out-the-money. When a call option is in-the-money, it means that the strike price is lower than the stock price while when a call option is out-the-money, the strike price is higher than the stock price.

For example

If a call TOP strike is $200 and the immediate or current trading price is $230, this means this option is in-the-money.

On the other hand, it is completely reversed, when a strike price is higher than a stoke price the put is in-the-money and when the stock price is higher than the strike price, the put is out-the-money.

For example

When a TOP put has a strike price of $50 while the current trading price is $100 the put is out-the-money, alternatively, when the TOP put has a strike price of $100 and the current trading price is $50, this put is in-the-money.

The in-the-money options have higher values than the options that are out-the-money.

An option is either a call or a put.

A call option gives the buyer the right to buy the stock at a specified price in a specified time frame.

A Put option allows the seller to sell the underlying asset at a specified price in a specified time frame.

Long a call and short a put options increases in value when the market prices go up, while long a put and short a call options reduce in value when the market prices decrease.

Dividends

Dividends are earned from the company by stock owners. Options do not earn dividends; this means their value drops when dividends are released. During the dividend earning period, the stock reduces by the amount of the dividend. Call options values decrease and are mostly out-the-money when dividends increase while put options values increase and are mostly in-the-money during this period. Despite the Black Scholes model having so many assumptions like stock prices following a log-normal distribution, risk-free interest being constant in all the matured stocks, the permission of selling all the securities using proceeds and the fact that there is risk without arbitrage opportunities, it is still considered the most widely used model. From all the factors listed above, volatility is an estimated factor; on the other hand, interest and dividends have very little effect on the option's value.

Trading Against Momentum

Momentum Trading

This a method in which traders, these are buyers and sellers, buy the assets and sell them according to the recent trending prices. It is just like the momentum in physics whereby when the mass of the object is multiplied by the velocity, there is a likelihood that the object may or might remain on the same path. However, in financial markets, the momentum of prices or trade is influenced by other factors. The traders here, the buyers and the sellers always think that the asset moving in a certain direction or trending in a certain direction will continue doing so until the trend loses the strength. For example, an asset moving in the upward trend is believed by the traders in momentum that it will continue following that trend until it loose strength and the likelihood of retracing are not there and oppositely when the asset is moving in a downward trend it will continue doing so until it loses the strength of the trend.

Factors influencing Momentum trading

- Volume
- Rate Prices

Types of Momentum

Relative Momentum

In this strategy, the performance of different securities of different classes is analyzed and then compared against each other to find out the strong performing ones and the weak performing ones. Most of the traders tend to sell weak performing securities and buy strong performing securities.

Absolute Momentum

Unlike in relative where the strength of the security is measured, in absolute momentum, the current behavior of the prices of the securities is compared against the previous behavior of securities serially.

Momentum Indicators.

These are tools that help determine the direction of a certain asset. These are more like graphic devices especially the oscillators that their main objective is to help point out how fast the prices of particular assets are moving and in which direction and if they are likely to remain in this direction.

The tool tries to explain that the speed of the price movement reaches its highest limit when there is new money in the trade or the new investors in the trade are near the peak. It is simple to get the direction of momentum, you simply subtract the previous price from the current price, if you happen to get a positive result, this only means the momentum is positive traders can make their entry into the trade, but if you subtract and get a negative result, this means the momentum is negative, and the trader who is in trade can exit, and the one that is not in trade can wait.

The momentum tools are ROC, rate-of-change indicators. These tools divide the previous prices and then multiply them, dividing 100 to give them their percentage form. The traders can now use these percentages to plot the high and low trends in the trend charts. If the ROC reaches the highest point of the high trend or the lowest point of the low trend, there is a very high probability there will be a change in price and price reversals are more likely to happen.

The indicators include:

Moving Averages

These can be simple moving averages or the Exponential moving averages. They are simply calculated by adding the closing prices over a period then dividing them by the number of the period. While doing this the traders should look at the average results, if the averages are going down this means the momentum is negative and when the averages are going up, this means that the momentum is positive.

Relative strength Index

This is self-defined just as the names says. It involves measuring the strength of the current prices over a certain period against the previous recent prices. It aims to show whether the current trend as in performance is stronger than the previous performance.

Stochastic

This tool compares the assets' range and their current prices over a specific period. If the trend lines happen to reach point of where the extra sales have reached on the trend chart, also called the oversold condition, this means the price momentum is high, but if the trend lines happen to reach the level at which the most bought are, also called the overbought, this means the price momentum is low, and traders can make their exit or entry when they want to.

Building blocks

This tool works in a way that traders divide the existing chart into equal periods. The periods re then put into blocks. These blocks can be color-coded differently, for example, green, Red, blue. The green can represent the upward trend; the red can represent the downward trend, while the blue can represent the sideways trend. If the blocks at any given time try to show two-block with the same color consecutively, this only means one thing, there is a moment in that given direction.

On Balance Volume (OBV)

This tool works by comparing prices to the trade volume. It is seen that when the trade is in large volume and the price doesn't change much or is not changing at all, this means there is a strong price momentum, but then this principle says that if trade volumes decrease, then it implies there is a weak price momentum.

The other indicators of momentum are:

- Commodity Channel Index – CCI
- Stochastic Momentum Index –SMI
- Average Directional Index –ADI
- Moving Average Convergence Divergence –MACD

We have looked at momentum and how most of the traders look at its positivity before making an entry. Most of the buyers and sellers make sure they work with Momentum. However, some other traders find it easier and relaxing trading against momentum.

Richard Driehaus, the founding father of momentum, believed in buying high and selling high. He believed in selling the losers rather than having the winners continue being in trade waiting for the re-evaluation of the market before selling them off. He believed that instead of waiting for the winners and the market re-evaluation, it is better for you to sell the loser and invest that money in another trade that is currently in the market and is doing well.

Trading against moment takes advantage of the level of how volatile the market is in that the asset, in this case, the stock is sold immediately it shows any sign of going down and then trader moves money and invests in another trade that has trended on the market. It is like a horse rider with horses running in turns. Once he rides a horse after some time and feels that the horse is going to slow any time from now because of tiredness, he leaves that horse and starts riding a new one or another one before he falls from the tired horse, so the trader remains the race for long without going down ready to take any other horse if the one he has starts to show any signs of tiredness.

The Elements

- **Selection**

A trader must always make sure to select the stocks according to the trend. You cannot select the high lows and expend to sell them when the trend is going up; this would not work and vice versa for the high highs, low highs, low lows.

- **Risk**

A trader must understand the risks involved in trading against momentum. This risk most often revolves around timing, the entry, and the exit. If a trader messes up the timing, then he is bound to incur massive losses.

- **Entry timing**

The trader must make sure to get into the trade early to catch the momentum as it moves

- **Position management**

The holding time of an asset by the trader is vital here. He must be able to know when trading it.

- **Exit points**

When exiting the trade, a trader must have marked the trend on chart well because exiting when it is not yet time is likely to cost the trader.

- **Catch the Wave**

This theory was coined by Ralph Nelson Elliot, which is commonly known as the Elliot wave principle. The Elliot wave principle begins at analyzing the patterns of waves in the charts. The trends before any trader can plunge into business. The Elliot wave has both impulsive waves and collective waves.

Impulsive Waves

This is waves that move in the same way with the trend of the next large size. They are five sub-waves in total, namely, 1-2-3-4-5 or i-ii-iii-iv-v. In impulse waves, there are that can't be broken because if they are wrong results of marking the trend will be achieved. According to Elliot:

- Wave 2 can never retrace more than 100% of wave 1.

Wave 1 travels a distance of 38% -78% which now is the retracement level wave 2.A stopping point of wave 2 is nearly 62% or 61.8%, whereby it sometimes retraces up to a 78% though it is not so common. Traders here enters the wave when it is t 38%-78% retracement level and tries to put a stop loss at the start of the wave. When you see wave 2 retracing more than 100% of wave 1, this is wrong, and maybe the labeling is not correct, for wave 2 retracement can never go up to 100% of wave 1.

- Between waves 1, 3 and 5, wave 3 can never be shortest.

Many times it is the longest. During wave 1, this means the starting of the new trend and the traders have not learned about it, it moves out quickly and goes to wave 2. In wave 2, there is a retracement to wave 1 were most of the participants are still waiting for the trend to puck and not so many of them make their entry. In wave 3, this is when the participants decide to come believing they have clearly understood the trend. This now when wave 3 becomes the strongest and longest of waves 1, 3, 5. However, wave 3 is not a must to be the longest wave, but it can never be shorter than wave 1.

- The wave 4 can never be overlapped by wave 1.

Most of the time wave 4 works oppositely of wave 2, so if we have the sequence, the trends can be well marked, and traders can make their entry at wave 4 with the anticipation of wave 2.

These are the rules of the impulse wave, and they can never be otherwise unless something has gone wrong or the trend has taken another direction that we are not sure of.

Corrective Wave

This wave moves in the opposite direction of the trend the next trend size that is larger than the one it is moving with or has moved with. This simply means it is moving against.

Just like in the ocean, a business can be compared to surfing, and as it is known, a rising tide lifts all ships. Everyone in the ocean must move according to the wave movement. When the tides go down, the surfer makes sure of his stability not to drown, and when the tides go up, he goes up too. Everyone here is trying to catch the wave of prospering even a very minimal percentage in this business. Sometimes traders have to sit and wait for quite some time for the wave to come and wash them off to the side of the trade and save them and sometimes the wave washes them to the ugly side of the trade and massive losses are witnessed. Sometimes some traders ask themselves why the wave did not save them and take them to the shore, but they forget they did not consider the following;

Reading the ocean

In the ocean a rookie who sees swells in the ocean and the waves are forming tides then runs to the ocean is very different from an expert surfer who looks keenly at the waves and knows the time to surf. Same as in business, you must know when it is time to enter or exit the business to get the help of the wave or run from it.

Inspect your equipment

In the ocean, your equipment, which is the surfboard, is the most important thing. You should make sure it is big enough, strong enough to handle a big wave for if it is broken or not good enough then you will surely be the first one to suffer. Just like in the business, how well prepared are you with your stocks to face the price waves when the support and resistance levels are hit? Is your business able to handle the Exponential growth during the influx orders or it will go down first before any other and make you lose clients? These are the things that will make you be well prepared in your business to avoid loses and in the ocean to avoid sinking or to go to the peak.

Get The Right Equipment

Which gear are you having? That is a seller's question. A safer, faster surfer always has the right gears. In this case, in business, the right gear is the policies, the procedures, and the controls. The trader should focus on what is needed to bring onboard the expected results, and I know the expected results of every trader is to make profits and remain in the business. The right gear will help in the standardization and utilization of workers' strengths profitably.

Learn How to Surf

Every rookie surfer must learn slowly. He must start by taking on small waves before going to the big waves. The rookie must practice his skills well, start slowly then faster, small waves being the first ones, then after, now the surfer, no longer a rookie can take on big waves with major tides and will still be able to balance on this surfing board because of enough practice he has had. Same as in business, the traders must first study the skills in the trade. Skills like accounting, finance, management, simple audits must be learned while in the rookie stage not while taking on the big wave. The information can be found in magazines, online, books, or attend classes. In the ocean, the lack of preparation will cause drowning and eventually death at times and the same. In the you safely to the shore business, it is the same; lack of preparedness may make the wave so big on your business and land you either so low or high. So business people should prepare in advance so that when you turn around and see the wave coming towards you, you will not run and hide, but you will take your equipment, the right gears and leap on it to take

Advantages of Catch the Wave

- **Price targets**

Elliot's wave theory or catch the wave principle helps the traders set the prices because of its predictability

- **Point ruins**

This principle points out clearly when there is time for failure and thus prepares the trader not to enter that trade and also prepares the one into exit when the ruin has not yet happened.

- **Specific Trading Opportunities**

When using this principle, it is like being sent to pick either of fresh food or stale food from the food draw. This principle helps any trader who is observing the waves to be able to choose specifically when to enter the trade or when to make his exit. So this trade specifically gives out opportunities to trade at specific periods.

- **Set Protective Tops**

When the traders have identified the waves and know the trend, they know which wave next is going to be productive or down; thus, they can set protective tops early before the fall.

Disadvantages

- ### Uncertainty

This theory of waves is very uncertain. One could be waiting for the wave to end so that they can enter business with loss stoppers with the assumption of the trend being picked and trade having an upward trend might continue only to meet the bigger loses when they enter the business which might even drown them.

- ### Vague

A trader cannot identify when the first wave has begun as it is a new trend and even some traders can't still know about the Wave until at the mid or end of it, and this makes it not so helpful when a trader wants to enter in a wave.

- ### Lack of Quantification.

There is no clear quantification through waves, 1, 2, 3, 4 and 5. The numbers or figures just have ranges; for example, the wave 2 retracement level is between 38%-785. There is no specific percentage as to which it retraces.

Chapter 3: Why Options Trading Is Better Than

Stock Trading

Before we embark on this journey of trading the options, we must first understand what it means.

Options

This is the rights given to a buyer or a seller to buy the underlying asset or sell the underlying asset without being obligated to it in a specified period and at a specified price. Options are usually two.

Types of Options

The Call Option

The call option is when a buyer is given the right or the go-ahead to buy the underlying asset at a specified price in a specified time without obligation.

The Put option

This is where a right is given to the seller to sell their underlying asset in a specified time at a specified price but without being obligated to it.

It should be very clear that option doesn't earn dividends, only the stock owners earn dividends. If a trader is to trade with options, he should be very keen when timing in the trend chart whether to buy, hold, or put an option up for sale. When the market prices increase the call options increases, and when the market prices decrease, the put options increases.

By now am sure you are wondering what I just said, let me make it simpler, the put option operates in the opposite way of the call option. So basically, options trading is the buying of calls and selling of puts at a specified time and specified prices without being obligated to them because all the ownership is with the stock owners in the company by looking at the entry times and the exit times. The options, whether exercised or not once they hit the expiration period, then the rights are withdrawn.

Stock

It is commonly known as the underlying asset. Why?

Because stock is a type of security that shows ownership in corporations' assets or earnings. People call stock, shares. The stock has two primary types known as the:

Common Stock

In this stock, shareholders are given the ownership rights and rights to share in the profits by the company when there is an increase in the company shares for quite some time or overtime and also through dividends issuance. All owners of common stock receive the same dividends per share. Dividends are only discussed and decided upon by the corporations' board of directors. Note that not all companies issue dividends.

Preferred Stock

This stock is different from common stock in that the shareholders in this stock are given different rights from the shareholders in the common stock. Here the preferred stock owners have no right to vote and also while the common shareholders receive dividends upon the board of directors' decision, the preferred stock owners' dividends are fixed. They are entitled to the dividends no matter what and this can only change if the company may be facing a major downward trend, whereby the dividends will still be paid to them in arrears if the company's trend changes and go upwards and in case the company is closing, the preferred stock owners are always the first ones to be given their shares than the common stockholders.

Collectively, stock trading is the buying and selling of both common stock and preferred stock in the stock exchange market, to the public and over the counter. It is the art of being in this business of stock. If any traders want to enter in this trade of stocks, the first requirement is to open an account with the brokers like the interactive brokers and from there start buying and selling thousands of shares of a public company.

Factors Affecting Option Trading

Stock prices/Underlying prices

The marketable options have different valuation than non-marketable options. For instance, if a call option allows a buyer to buy a stock at a specified price, which is lower than that of the future price, then the option is more worthy.

For example:

An option call allows an investor to buy The Option Prophet (TOP) for $200 while it is trading at $150 An option call allowing a buyer to purchase a TOP at 150 when it is trading at $100

The first one will have a lower value for no buyer is going to purchase an option at a higher price than the trading period.

Most of the buyers will go for the second choice for it is more appealing. Buying an option at a lower price than the trading price whereby the value will be high.

Strike Prices/Exercising Price

Strike prices are categorized differently as in-the-money, at-the-money, or in-the-money. When a call option is in-the-money, it means that the strike price is lower than the stock price while when a call option is out-the-money, the strike price is higher than the stock price.

For example

If a call TOP strike is $200 and the immediate or current trading price is $230, this means this option is in-the-money. On the other hand, it is completely reversed, when a strike price is higher than a stoke price the put is in-the-money and when the stock price is higher than the strike price, the put is out-the-money. The in-the-money options have higher values than the options that are out-the-money.

Interest Rates

When the interest rates are high, the call option goes high too, while the Put Option goes down. However, interest rates have very little effect on the options. When interest rises, the call options are a good investment, and when it drops the put option is the best. The rise in interest of the call option, makes the call option be in-the-money while the put option out-the-money and a decrease in the interest, a call option is an out-the money and a put option is in-the-money.

Time to Expiration

When an investor exercises the option for a longer period, there are greater chances for it to be in-the-money at the time expiration period. Options lifespan is limited. When an Option has a long time before expiration, its value increases, but if an option has less time to its expiration, its value decreases because it doesn't have enough time to go around in the market.

Volatility

When an underlying asset has high volatility, it is more likely to end in-the-money during the expiration period. Volatility cannot be observed directly because it is impossible, so it can only be estimated or implied. The volatility used here is the forward volatility. The forward volatility is the result of the measure of implied volatility after a specified period in the future.

The implied volatility now shows the movement in the stocks' future volatility. It helps tell the thinking of traders about the stock price movements.

The higher the implied volatility, the more people think the stock prices are going to move. Implied volatility is expressed in percentage form, and it is done annually. Value stocks have lower implied volatility unlike the growth stocks or small caps which have high implied volatility because small caps move around a lot, unlike value stocks which do not move much.

Factors Affecting Stock Trading

Economics

Economic factors either stabilize the stock market or destabilizes it by moving the growth down or up. Factors like inflation, unemployment, economic growth, and interest rates can move the stock markets majorly. They can create a way that the markets can survive from or drown. When the economic growth is high, there are high profits, and if the profits are high, the stock value increases, but when it goes down, there is an alarm in the stock market. The declining interests send the stock markets higher, but when the interests go high, the market falls. On the other hand, high inflation works the complete opposite, when there is high inflation, there is likely hood of high interests shortly or immediately, and this slows down the economic growth which reduces prices and thereafter reduces the stock value. When there is failing unemployment, this means growth is on the way, but if the unemployment is rising, this is a danger sign which is lowering the economic growths.

Politics

Political stability brings in more investors in the stock markets and not only in the stock market but in general trade but in this case, we talk about the stocks. When there is stability, economic growth goes up, and this means more profits, which increases the stock value.

Disasters

These can be either man-made or natural disasters.

- Man-made disasters

If a self causing a disaster like fraud happened or a power shortage in power companies, or bursting of an oil refinery company due to the human hand, whether by negligence or incompetence, these actions will bring down the stock market growth both in terms of price and value. They will both go down drastically.

- Natural Disasters

If a Tsunami came and washed away all or most of the offices in a heavily loaded economic town, the stocks will go down and might take time to recover or might never recover at all.

Market Psychology

In stocks markets, there is predictability of prices going up, but also there are uncertainties, there comes a time when every trader especially the swing traders want to buy and there comes a time in the market when every trader is panic-stricken, and all they want to do is sell their underlying assets.

Having analyzed a lot about option trading and stoke trading, the question is, why would trading with Options be better than trading with the stock? Below are the reasons:

Cost

Options are cheaper than stocks and thus saves the traders money. A trader can get an option position the same as the stock position with a cost lower than the cost of the stock. The options leveraging power is very high. Though it is not so easy, the trader must pick the right call to be able to go below the stock purchase price and save some money. This strategy is called stock replacement, and it is viable and coefficient.

Less Risk

Unlike in the stock, options require less financial commitments. When one buys an option, he is not obligated to the stocks; thus, when the stocks are suffering; he is likely not to suffer. He is not obligated to the stocks. Options are hedge dependents, and for this, it makes them less risky than stock. The stock owners receive stop-loss orders and put stop loss to the stocks if they are falling beyond the expected level. Stock orders are exercised only when the stock is trading below the expected trading levels.

Higher Returns

There are higher potential returns in options than in stocks. An option trader who spends less to acquire an option of the same position as that of a stock position will make money with reasonable profits while trading the options. Options having an expiry date also makes them sell out faster than stock; an option wouldn't want to hit the option expiry date without trading for this will be a loss to him, thus the more the options trade, the more the money comes in.

Strategic Alternatives

Options are more flexible than stocks, and any trader would want to go for the flexible part. No trader wants to go into the business and stay in folding arms, waiting for the business to turn out well. In this case, options have an expiration period, so they are traded quickly and differently, a trader can always take the profits from his last sell and re-invest it in something else unlike in stocks where one has to sit and wait for the market.

Limited Losses

Option owe no obligation to the stocks; thus, their losses are limited in any case the stocks are hit. Also, the options don't earn dividends, so when the stock markets are down, and the dividends are reduced, this doesn't affect options in any way.

Time

Options time is limited. Options have an expiry period, and this is an added advantage for a trader to choose options trading over stock trading. Bearing in mind that one has an expiration time will make the person do everything possible to make a buy or sell their underlying asset and bring in more profits.

Chapter 4: Options Trading

The word options trading, as mentioned above, may sound so unique or familiar as you may get it. It has been in existence for quite enough time as we may imagine or even think. It was once used by several communities like the Greeks, Romans and the Phoenicians for trading their cargoes at their local seaports.

By Way Of Definition

As seen before, an option is simply a contract of two parties if used as a copy of any financial tool. The person buying and the person selling whereby the one buying has an inherent right but not the obligation of buying or even selling the asset in question at any given market price whatsoever.

Types of Options

We can talk about the call and the put being so far the known types of options today. It is imperative for one to understand both of them, how they operate, and their uniqueness, their merits, and their demerits. In this case, we are not going to feature so much on the way each option works, but instead, we are going to concentrate so much on the merits and their demerits. But just, in a nutshell, we will highlight something on both of them.

In the call option, the buyer is given the right to purchase the asset at the stated price within an agreed time interval. Then the person selling the option is expected to issue a long position in the principal futures as the contract at the expected price if the person buying the option agrees to exercise that option. As opposed to calling option, put option the buyer of the option gets the right, yet is not obligated to sell the option in question at the given price whatsoever at the stated or agreed time frame. Instead, the seller of that very option has the obligation of providing precisely the standing from the current price if the buyer at whatever cost decides to exercise the option.

It is very easy to understand why most investors trade in stock. The trade is very simple to carry out, and the profit realized is always good. This explains why other financial instruments are not as popular as stock trading.

Options offer a great alternative to stock. They cost less and offer you higher leverage in terms of risk reduction and profit. Generally, the buyer of an option has the right to purchase an underlying stock, and the seller is obligated to release the stock at a specific price and date. Most people believe that trading in options is a complicated process. However, options do have several benefits that stock does not. Today, we look at some of the main reasons why you should trade-in options, as well as the few disadvantages of this financial instrument.

Advantages

Options trading has been in existence since the early 1970s. Over the years, trading in options has been viewed as a risky investment that can only be done by Forex trading experts. However, there are several reasons why traders should get interested in the options business. Some of these include:

Cost Efficiency

When trading options, there is potential for making large profits from the business, using small amounts of capital. It is because of this that most investors trade options as an alternative or addition to stock trading. Even beginners with little to start off can benefit from the trade if equipped with the right information and strategies.

You can get an option position that is similar to a stock position at relatively low costs. For instance, if you want to buy 100 shares of stock sold at $80 per share, you will need $8000 for it. But if you wish to buy two calls each at #20, the premium will only be $4000 for the same amount of stock since each call represents 100 shares. You will, therefore, be able to save $4000 that you can invest elsewhere or leave in your account to generate interest. However, to succeed in this, you will need to choose the right calls to buy so as to gain profit from it.

Cost efficiency is definitely an advantage that investors can leverage to generate large incomes from their capital. It is one of the options benefits that is missing in most of the other financial instruments, including stocks. By taking a position on an underlying security, you will be able to cut investment costs and make some profits at the same time.

Passive Income

Some strategies used in options trading allow you to make a monthly income from it. The Covered Call strategy, for example, gives you the opportunity to buy a stock then earn some premium by selling calls from the stock to other traders. By doing this, you retain your stock but still make some profit on the side.

Options trading strategies help you take advantage of the market determinants like time decay and volatility. You can use them to create income from all market directions yet with unlimited gain. For instance, you may purchase call options if the market is bullish and do so for put options when the market is bearish to maximize your profits on the upside and downside, respectively.

You may also include other spread strategies such as selling straddles, iron condors, and credit spreads to make the most from the market.

Reduced Risk

Just like any other financial investment, there are various risks involved in options trading. For most investments, it is always assumed that the higher the returns, the higher the risks involved. This is not the case with the options business. Here, the risk-reward ratio is significantly balanced since it is possible to make high returns from small investments. The risk involved in the trade is minimal compared to the reward.

When it comes to trading options, various techniques are used, and each of them has a certain level of risk. The good thing is that as a trader, you get to choose the level of risk you want to take. For each options contract that you sign and the orders you place, you can easily make a balance to lower the risks involved.

The more you learn about the trade, the more you will understand how easy it is to overcome most of the risks. Your success in the business partly depends on this. However, you must understand that whatever risk is involved in options is quite low as compared to the risk of trading your stock or underlying securities directly. The only common risk with options is losing your initial deposit, also known as the premium.

If you control your contracts with accuracy, you can always make a profit from the trade. For example, if you own 1,000 shares of a certain company and you think that the prices may go down in future, you can get 10 options and trade them at a profit instead of selling off your shares. This way, you will save your stock from declining market prices. Some long-term equity anticipation procedures allow you to do this for a period of up to two years.

Predefined Risk

The strategies used in options trading allow you to calculate the maximum risk involved in each contract. This is a great advantage to options traders because you are able to anticipate your profits or losses beforehand. It gives you the confidence required in the trade since you would already have taken away the fear of the unknown. By spreading your trades and adjusting the size of your strikes, you will be able to minimize potential losses accordingly.

When starting up, setting up some risk management strategies can be difficult. As time goes by and you get familiar with the basics of trading, you will easily set up a combination of strategies to maximize every opportunity to make money.

By now, you have understood how options can limit your risks as you make unlimited profits. As a trader, you only have a right and not an obligation to engage in a trade. When the cost of an option is not good at expiration time, the buyer forfeits the right, in this case, the premium, allowing the contract to expire worthlessly.

Generally, options require less financial equity than other financial instruments. Although they are more dependable than stock, the level of risk involved depends on how you trade. If you are a careless trader, you will end up risking more, and losing a lot. However, you can use the stop-loss order feature to prevent you from losing beyond a certain percentage of your premium. This order restricts the trade from going beyond the indicated limit and may save you from incurring big losses.

Let's say you purchase stock at $50 but do not want to lose more than 10% of this. You can place a $45 order to sell your option when the trade hits the $45 mark.

Options are known for their high returns. When they pay off, the profits are good.

Versatility

One great characteristic of options is the flexibility that comes with the trade. This feature gives you several opportunities to make money from the options market. Options are traded in the form of contracts that can give you either passive or active income, in several ways. There are several strategies that you can use to make money from the options market. For instance, if you want to trade options on long-term, you can choose underlying stocks that have the potential of increasing in cost over time. If you are in the business on a short-term basis, you can get stocks that are able to give you regular returns.

The options trade allows you to combine more than one strategy so as to achieve more. This allows you to secure your investments from loss and helps you to increase your profits. The more you learn the trade, the more advanced the strategies become. For any strategy that you apply, you must first find out if there are any limitations involved. The most basic strategy used in options trading is by purchasing call options when the price is likely to increase and purchasing put options when the price has the potential to decline. With the right strategies in place, you can easily identify what trades to invest in and also determine the best time to trade.

The flexibility of the options market is also increased by the fact that you can purchase and sell options based on a large number of underlying securities. These can range from commodities, stocks, indexes, and many others. You can easily study market patterns to determine the price movement of these assets as you take advantage of every opportunity to make profitable trades. For example, if you have solid knowledge in foreign exchange, you can use it to trade options based on predictable foreign exchange rates.

Another feature that boosts the flexibility of options is the use of spreads. These help you limit the downside of trade, reduce the initial capital amount, and make money from price movements in over one direction. Spreads can also be used to salvage contracts whose end is a definite loss or make money from a market whose prices are not changing.

You can use the versatile nature of options for the purpose of hedging and for making profits from both sides of the trade. This can be achieved through most strategies involving the basic call and put options. If you are a beginner, you should focus on the simple strategies first before employing advanced ones which combine call and put strategies in one trade.

You can also use existing options to create other trade positions known as synthetic positions. These positions offer you an array of opportunities to meet your profit goals. Although these are only used by options trading experts, they provide you with a great alternative to ordinary trading strategies. An example of this is when an investor works with a broker to buy stock from the seller, and the broker charges a small percentage as his payment. This fee can limit profits. Some investors will refuse to work with brokers, thus getting a good price for the stock, making a profit from it. The refusal by investors to work with brokers handcuffs most sellers, forcing them to hit the market on their own, thus offering some assets at better prices.

Options also allow you to make a profit from a stagnant market where the prices are not moving in any direction. This is possible because, in options trading, you not only make money from the changing prices but also from the changes in time and volatility of the underlying security. Actually, most stocks rarely change in price. Investors use other factors to achieve their trading goals.

Options and Leverage

When trading options, you can buy or sell 100 shares against every options contract you initiate. You can easily control these shares without investing a large capital or premium since the capital required to trade an option is often less than the cost of purchasing the number of stock shares involved.

For example, you will need $5,000 to purchase 100 shares each going at $50. However, if you decide to buy an option for this share, you can spend as little as $500 for the same number of shares. This gives you an opportunity to:

- Trade-in large amounts of the underlying stock, which is not applicable if you buy the shares directly
- Multiply your profits as the prices change in your favor
- Make larger profits on small amounts of capital

When you purchase an options contract, you are actually not buying anything since no shares will be transferred to you. You only deal with a small percentage of the underlying security. There is no transfer of assets until the buyer decides to exercise the contract. Since the value of the contract is determined by the underlying asset, a small change in the price of the asset together with other factors such as volatility and time can generate good income. In most cases, the contract is determined by the number of contracts multiplied by the contract size, which differs for each type of option. In the United States, the standard contract size is 100 shares. This implies that for every option contract you get into, you have the right, not the obligation to purchase 100 shares from the seller at the expiration date of the contract. Small investors take advantage of this benefit to trade in some lucrative asset options with good returns using very little capital.

Options and Time

With options, you do not have to watch the market all day to make a profit from a trade. Unlike other instruments that only use the buy and hold strategy, options allow you to spread your contracts across favorable price movements. This is commonly referred to as out-of-the-money trading. In this strategy, the trader starts an options contract with the hope that the price will increase. If the probability of success is high, then the trader does not need to monitor the trade, especially if it is a long-term contract. This strategy, however, does not work with aggressive trades with shorter expiration periods since there is not sufficient time for the prices to build up. Options give you the change to select the duration of your contract. You can, therefore, select weekly or monthly contracts depending on how much time you want to spend on the trading platform. This means that if you have more time within one week, you can make weekly trades, and if you have limited time to spend on the trade, you can get contracts with longer time periods. Note that the profits and risks involved in each trade will vary based on your trading plan.

Disadvantages of Trading Options

Just like other financial instruments, options possess some disadvantages, or risks that you may need to consider before joining the trade. However, these are minimal as compared to the many profits discussed above. Options allow you to benefit from the value of underlying security without having to own it. This is why options are slowly becoming popular as a financial investment tool.

Trading in options is no longer a business for Forex experts. Startup investors, as well as home traders, are getting into the business because of the many opportunities it offers in terms of making money. The deal isn't without some risks, though.

Mastering options trading is not an easy task. Unlike stock trading, you need to learn a lot in terms of the basics, as well as the strategies required to succeed in the game. This is one of the reasons why some of the investors still avoid trade. The trading process is not as straightforward as other trades, and a lot of factors are used to determine the profits you can make from a contract. You, therefore, need a lot of time to learn the market and understand how things are done.

Generally, here are some of the common challenges that options traders encounter in the trade.

- High Loss Potential

Every investor gets into options trading with the aim of making money. However, the success of any trade depends on the changes in prices, effects of time, and how volatile the underlying asset is. This has made many investors realize relatively low or no profits at all in the past.

Trading in options can become risky, especially for those who do not have any experience in the financial field. Although options can be used to limit the risk involved, trading without the necessary strategies can lead to total disappointment and loss.

The whole trading process is quite complicated for beginners. Most traders, including those who have been in the business for some time, may think that they have understood a concept on options when they have not. Factors such as volatility are very sensitive, and if a trader does not consider such in the process of trading, he may expect to win, but lose in the end.

As you trade-in options, you must learn not to hold onto trades that are likely to go against you. Holding on such options until expiration can make you lose all your investments.

- **Taxes and Commissions**

Options trading profits are often taxed in the category of short-term capital gains. This means that your returns will be taxed just like any other income. Depending on your country of residence, these taxes may be high or low. Tax charges in some countries are as high as individual income tax. You can, however, trade-in an IRA or tax-deferred account although this does not work for all traders.

When it comes to commissions, the rates are often high, especially for weekly options. In some cases, investors have paid over 30 percent of their capital as a commission within one year. If you pay such amounts as commission and fail to realize higher profits, then you end up with no income from your investment. Before you start trading on any platform, find out how much they charge as commission so that you do not get frustrated along the way. Options trading commissions are often higher when spreads are involved. This is because you will pay for both the upside and the downside of the spread.

- **Fluctuations in Portfolio Value**

As stated in the advantages above, options allow you to leverage your returns. Portfolio value is used in the trade to signify the high fluctuations in prices both on the upside and downside of the trade. In most cases, traders find it hard to predict the direction of options since they are highly volatile. Some end up losing large amounts of money in the process, thus giving up.

- **Uncertainty**

When trading in options, traders use the risk profile graph to determine the potential profits and losses at contract expiration. Generally, these graphs provide clear information on what to expect, and you can use them to determine when to exercise an option. The downside is that the graphs are never 100 percent accurate, and in most cases, traders do not realize the estimated profits once a contract expires. This is because the software used in these predictions does not put into consideration the option's volatility. Sudden changes in the price of the underlying commodity, therefore, cause a tremendous impact on the options pricing, causing a huge difference between what is predicted and the resultant profits.

- **Lower Liquidity and Higher Spreads**

Options lack liquidity. They do not have much in terms of volume. Since options trade at different strike prices and expiration dates, it is very likely to get very little from an options contract unless the underlying asset is very popular. Due to this, small investors may take a lot of time to realize significant profits in the options market.

Because options lack liquidity, they normally involve the use of higher spreads, which can cost you more should the market direction work against your expectations. One important thing you must note about options is that they are available for a limited number of stocks. This can limit you in terms of variety, thus limiting your profits.

Leverage

Besides losing every cent in options trading, you are at risk of losing all your money if you keep writing naked options that are likely to go against you. Although leverage has been mentioned as an advantage of trading options, it can cause you to lose your investments as quickly as you made them. To avoid this, you should be careful about selling puts or naked calls or engaging any risky trading strategies.

Options Trading Language

Options trading terminologies can be a barrier for you if you are not willing to learn them before investing in the market. There are several terms involved in each trade, and you must be conversant with them in order to make good profits. Some of the terms include:

☐ Call and Put, which are the most basic

☐ In the money

☐ Out of the money

☐ Expiration date

☐ Exercise

☐ Bullish or bearish markets

☐ Strike price

☐ Underlying security

To make matters worse, different brokers will use different terms to refer to the same thing.

For instance, a bull put spread, and a put credit spread refer to the same strategy. A bear call spread and a short call spread also refer to one thing. Options also offer numerous choices in terms of strategy, trading styles, and risk management techniques. These can be a disadvantage, especially to beginners who do not know where to begin. Having several alternatives that you are not familiar with can make you lose confidence in the trade since you may not be sure which strategy to use at what time, and for what purpose.

Each trade often has a wide array of factors to consider to make some returns. Failure to incorporate all of them in a contract may have a huge negative impact on the outcomes of each trade. These many options make the trade quite overwhelming.

Expiration of Options

One major disadvantage of options is that they expire at the end of the trading period. This means that you can no longer access them. At the end of the expiration date, you either get a profit or loss. For this reason, you must employ as much strategy as possible to ensure that you gain from your contracts. Once time runs out, you will feel I wasted if your trade has not made you any profit.

Options comprise of a premium and intrinsic value. How these two variables change in the course of the trade determine the outcome of it. That is why you need to consider the expiration time of any contract before investing in it. There are times that you may make the right predictions in terms of the pricing and stand a chance of making profits but lose them because of the contract expiring too soon.

Time shortage is the reason why a good number of traders still prefer stocks over options. With stock trading, you do not worry about expiry since the stocks last as long as you own the shares of a certain company or asset.

Most stock options expire on the third Friday of the last month of the contract. You are allowed to exercise your options on or before this date but not after.

Moreover, options only exist for the period that the underlying stock is available for trade. Most stock companies have specific months that they trade options in. This mostly happens in three fixed cycles of four months each.

Options and Time Decay

The more you hold on options, the more their value decreases. Unlike stock trading where you can hold on the shares for years without compromising the price, options tend to expire too quickly, and as the expiration date draws closer, the probability of getting profit from the contract also declines. Since there is no exception to this, traders have to ensure that they get the most out of a contract before the option's value wastes away. Failure to do this allows the contract to expire worthlessly.

Comparing the advantages and disadvantages of options trading, it is indisputable that this is an investment that has more benefits than risks. This explains why the financial instrument has become a center of attraction in the trading industry. Nonetheless, the decision to invest in options entirely depends on you. In case you are new in the trade, online brokers can easily provide the information and guidance required to get you started.

Before engaging any of them, do some research and choose one that charges reasonable commissions. Once you master the business, you can start trading by yourself to avoid unnecessary expenses. To learn how to trade, you must commit some time to study platforms and understand applicable strategies. It is more profitable trading as an individual than working through a broker. Remember, the ultimate goal is to make the highest returns from your investment, with little effort and risk. The disadvantages outlined above should not discourage you. Every financial instrument has its own strengths and weaknesses. In most cases, the advantages do outweigh the disadvantages.

Chapter 5: Developing a Swing Trading Master Plan

This is actualizing the swing trading concept. There are a series of steps that we need to walk through in order to understand and familiarize how exactly swing trading is carried out. Therefore as soon as you understand the basic concept of swing trading that's the general overview, you will now be able to introduce the rules that govern the whole concept on how to join and even how to leave the swing trading positions. And that's what we refer to as the master plan.

Opening an Account

An account is opened online through a broker. This is the very initial step you should take in entering the swing trading option. The account should be at least one that offers relative commission discount, not as those of common-all time brokers. This is very imperative basing on the level of the capital that you wish to invest and hence the relative stocks that you may wish to follow. You could be able to make 5, 6 or even more of round trips on trades in a week insinuating that the commission costs can go up very fast even when you are receiving just a preferred rate.

By setting up your account online, ensure that it's well approved for the margin trading. This is a prerequisite before you allowed to sell the stocks short. It s a fundamental aspect for a successful swing trading game. Similarly, you wish to sit back and evaluate if you truly wish to trade on the margin let's say borrowing a portion of that stock bought from the brokers.

There are advantages if one buys on margin for example:

1. Increases the leverage
2. Boosts the general buying power
3. Enables one to seize more opportunities In the same way, it portrays some limitations.
4. It involves some starting costs that's the interest is charged on borrowed funds
5. Having stocks on margin puts one on some increased pressure
6. Suppose the price of a margined stock goes high in an unexpected direction, then you will be a force to pump in an extra coin but if you don't have the amount right away to put up in order to close out the position at an undesirable price.

This is a great reason causing many market declines. It makes the trading day, to begin with, a pullback, even though the however good it maybe it may be so significant to cause some margin calls. When there is no liquidity, the traders who receive the calls are obligated to sell part of their shares, which in the long run sends the prices down further causing more margin calls.

Whether to trade on margins or not should be an individual decision done at a personal level. One should be able to know his or her own risk tolerance energy and his own financial situation at any particular moment in time. Therefore to swing trade, on need s to have an online account even if you do not make the trade on margin in the long run.

Money Management- An Overview

There are a series of issues that you would wish to confirm when or while opening you account that's closely related to the money management concept as well the way I which the broker companies allocates your money. If you are a starter, you have to ensure that your account has a sweep feature. This implies that the funds that have not been committed in opening trades should be automatically swept to money market account for it to earn some interest, even though in today's interest rate environment the impact is so minimal. In swing trading, good money management is very key. You may not be willing to assign a great percentage of your capital to a single position, for that alone will raise your percentage of risk factor. Similarly, you may not be willing to spread the working capital over many trades for this may lower the size of your position so that any profit acquired or realized maybe insignificant. This, in return, may amount to too much pressure exerted to you to make profits on almost all trades for you manage the general return. The more you gain experience in this business, you find a formula that can work for you well. If you are an experienced trader, you could divide your total capital by say 15 then allocate the amount to various single trades. As you take profits and the overall size of your accounts grow, so does the allocated amount s to individual trades. There is no specific formula for capital allocation of individual trades. It entirely depends on the amount of capital you have and are willing to invest. You can embark on three to four trades for a start at a time, hence ensuring your trade is of the same size but adding positions as profits from your prior trades increases on the size of your accounts.

If you are willing to improve on your swing trading, you may aim at increasing the number of trades open at any one given time say 10, 15 or 25. Although managing more than 15 positions are always a cumbersome to many people.

Whatever the number you decide to pick upon, you need to put in mind that the accounts must accommodate those trading styles. For instance, you can identify 20 or 25 candidates for the new swing trades daily. If you only have to say ten positions that are open, it means that you only have enough capital available for strictly five new trades. So you can pick the best ten outright candidates from such a list of 25 and place the orders there for all of them.

However not all orders may be filled, the reason being the price action though others will definitely and as long as there are five fills, having used all the capital on board, the broker will do away with all the remaining open orders. In that case, you will not be in any worry of running short of money or even dedicating more resources than the available funds.

How Do You Build A List Of Swing Trading Candidates?

As soon as your account is in place, it means that you are ready to go or take off in the trade as a swing trader. This now calls for the amassing of all stocks to monitor the entry for any upcoming opportunities. Stocks are ever priced in the same manner and eventually traded the same way; it means that all stocks groupings should do. There must be a few directives to this for effectiveness.

Swing trading involves normal buying and selling of stocks, hence at a considerably fair price or amount, you need to engage in stocks that portrays a great level of volatility.

Beta coefficient is a measure of volatility that can be evaluated by some analytical software. This helps gauge the rate and individual stock moves, that's to say In terms of price relative to the movement in S and P 500 index. Let's take an example of a stock with a Beta of 1.0, which is equal to the S&P 500. So if you have a Beta of 1.5, it means that you would be 50% more volatile compared to the index yet the one that has a Beta of 0.5 may move just halfway as you did before. Therefore for you to excel well, you need to probably align your swing trading candidates list to stocks that have a Beta of say 1.3 or even greater than that which in the long run may yield to greater growths and technology-related issues. Other than volatility, ensure that the candidate's stocks should have a reasonable wide trading range. You need to work with stocks that have good price levels for you to get more strength in the trading business. You also need t stick to stocks that decent daily trading volume. If you have a volatile stock that has a wide range between low and high prices in that very stock id does you no good for it may trade only a few shares a day. It may result into many difficulties in opening and closing the trades at prices you want; In addition, you may get troubled in buying enough shares so as to fulfill the money management requirements say enough shares to create enough profits in case the trade is successful. So it is recommended that one monitor for those stocks with daily aggregate by volume of about five hundred thousand shares.

Analysis software that aids in the analysis of information of the swing trading business should be able to guide you on getting the relevant information related to the swing trade called screening functionality. It works in a way that lets you enter your search criteria. It then runs them against the list of all the accessible stocks to verify the ones that can fulfill the criteria used. Other advisory boards do offer quality screening services and tools and the general knowledge on how to refine your search criteria for you to obtain the most out of the screening tools or software.

Process of Swing Trading

Ensure you put together in place a list of stocks to be monitored for the swing trading opportunities. After that, you embark on the process of identification and execution of the swing trades. It's not hard. We have a list of steps that can aid in the process.

1.   Once you have a list of the trading candidates, you can come up with the stocks which are already in an established trend systematically.

2.   Out of the established stocks in an uptrend manner, select the ones that are encountering a pullback. On top of that, the downward trend related stocks, find those that are staging a short term rally.

3.   Go for the most attractive predictions. In other words, the ones that seem to be emanating from short term pullback, a d enforce limit orders in order to make open your positions based on the features or guidelines from your master plan.

4.   As long as you successfully open your short or long positions, you need to put in place a stop-loss order to guard yourself of the severe price move as well be able

to regulate order to position at the required price that should give out the profit.

5.   Every close of business daily, you need to adjust the stop-loss order prices depending on the rules which are outlined in the master plan.

In A Nutshell

In swing trading, where an online broker various differences compared to other methodologies of trading, therefore, it is easy to come across things or concepts that are least expected.

•   You must never be nervous whenever your orders that you use to initiate the swing trade do not get filled. Recall that you may be applying for the limit orders only. If those orders, in this case, do not get filled, it could be that the market moved in the opposite direction as expected, hence not in need of the position. The rules as outlined in the master plan are specific for they are designed to allow just when the targeted stock price moves in the expected direction; but if it does not then there will be no entry to the trade.

•   If you are used to the ancient but working, buy and hold method of investment, in the first place you may find it worrisome to exit your positions as early as you hit your expectations. Many people have that tendency of holding on a given position until an alarm is raised and as such, it may be so negative resulting in wiping away all your profits resulting from the previous move. As opposed to that, swing trading is aimed at helping curb such moves in that; it identifies the size of the similar move upfront. It depends on the width of that trading range just within the primary trend, therefore capturing the profits soon as they are achieved. As soon as the profits are gotten, the swing trader does not lose any time contemplating over the speed at which he or she acted, but instead, he lays his focus on identifying the next point of action, i.e., the next opportunity and the whole profitable course.

• Except for the outrageous tendencies of trends to go on, and the keen identified rules put in place for playing swings, about the trends, part of it might result in to loses. When you go step by step on the guidelines found in the master plan, by adjusting the orders while the price keeps moving the direction of your choice, i.e., trailing, then you will be able to lower the risk of loses drastically. You need to be very patient and orderly in choosing your entry opportunities and also have enough discipline as you consider the exit rules and regulations hence the loss limits thus your profit-making trend will outdo the loss-making a trend.

The Entry and Exit Rules and Procedures

A master plan is simply a set of rules showing clearly under what circumstances and the timing that you should join and exit the swing trades. These rules in one way or the other seem to be complicated; however, as soon as you place some few trades, it simplifies the whole matter. One of the best features of the master plan is that personal judgment is not fully embraced for it uses mechanical aid in doing the judgment. At first, you may not be in agreement; however, it may yield to an advantage.

Human Emotions

This is a very great obstacle for success in any business or any trade and more specifically greed and fear of the unknown. This can be solved by the mechanical aspect as defined in the master plan. In this case, there are no emotions involved completely. Neither have any influence on the action plan of investment or does it in any way affect or impact your profits.

How to Join the Trade

The opportunities in the swing trading are ever identified at the close of the market depending on the patterns which entail the currents day's performance prices. You cannot be able to join the trade until the opening of trade the following trading day.

You must evaluate the price action of stock several minutes after the opening of the market, that's when you can now make up your mind on the time you need to join the market trade and also to determine the entry price. The challenge here is that if the stock that opened the day's trading was near the price of the previous day's closing range. Or maybe it had gapped downwards or upwards before the closing price.

Gapping Up

Basing on the definition used in the master plan, stock can be said to have gapped up only if it opens when it's higher than the last day's close by at least fifty cents.

Gapping Down

If it opens 50 cents or higher below the previous day's close, then we refer it to having gapped down.

Guidelines on Entering Trade Opening Orders

Considering the above definitions, we can now be able to view our guiding rules for entering trade opening orders:

i.   Whenever stock opens in a range of 50 cents of its previous day's close, you are supposed to place your order entry in a few minutes just soon after the opening of the market.

ii.   Assuming the stock gapped up by say 50cents or higher than that, from the previous day's close, then you need to wait at least 30 minutes after the opening of the market before you place in your entry order. You should take note that this concept only operates in abolish the trade.

iii.   If the stock gaps down, say by 50cents or even more, as compared to the previous close, when you need to place your entry order at close to 5minutes later when the market opens. It only applies when buying a stock. How to Set the Entry Price for the Swing Trade When to enter the trade or not, is entirely dependent on three factors as outlined below:

- Price of the stock at the point on initiation

- The trending of the market, i.e., gapped up or down.

Collectively, the price at a point when you are willing to initiate the swing trade is entirely dependent on it or not the stock gapped up or gapped down at the point of opening. In normal circumstances of a common market, prices neither gap up nor down during opening. Instead normally starts at a close range from the previous close levels. In that case, the limit price that you enforce is influenced by the close of the previous stock price level. Nevertheless, if the stock that you intend to buy or sell short, can gap lower or higher, then you must base the limit price that you set in the opening order basically on the existing prices. Considering these conditions, we can have the master plans rules that help in setting the limit price in that opening swing trade.

i.   Suppose the stock opens within the range of 50 cents of its previous date's trading close which is the common occurrence in the day today's market conditions, you must buy the stock immediately it trades at 6cents high above the prior days. It can be done by use of a buy stop order, and definitely increases the assumption that the stock shall be moving in the primary bullish trend.

ii.   If the stock gaps up or even down by saying 50 cents or even higher than that from the previous day's close, the stock needs to be bought as soon as it trades at 6 cents higher than the existing day's high. It should be achieved 30 minutes soon after the stock gaps up right at the opening or just 5minutes soon after it gaps down during the opening. As well this could be achieved by the use of a buy-stop order. In the case of a bearish trade, prices for the limit orders to sell short must be put at 6 cents below days' low currently. The orders must be placed at about 30minutes soon after gap-down-opening. Else 5 minutes soon after a 'gap up'- opening. In this version of trade, a sell-stop order can be used for initiation.

When to Exit?

When it comes to a long term investment, whenever a position is opened, you need to give gratitude, as you stay cool and relax for a period of your own choice say five months or even more hoping for a great miracle to happen — a surprise. Now, whenever you trade on swings; however, you do not need to be relaxed and wait for a surprise. Here you need to locate yourself on a platform to either grab the profit or aim at bailing out only if prices overturn to your anger and as well based on the master plans rules and guidelines.

The set rules are designed to support locking in of the profits by strongly putting off losses; this is aimed at preserving your committed capital. They are for sure really conservative as compared to guidelines put for other many short term trading levels.

1.   If we place a target profit of about 7% In bullish swing trade, we call this as putting a limit sell- order for a   price that's about 7% higher than the entry point whereas, in bearish swing trade, we are involved in the short sale of the stock, we refer this to as a buy-limit order with a price that's lower the entry point by 7%.

2.   Set a tentative stop-loss which restricts the risk exposure by 4% maximum

In the case of bearish trade, this implies that we put a buy stop order whereas we put a sell-stop order immediately in the case of bullish trades.

Did you open Your Trade? What Next?

The basic role of the master plan of a swing trader is to improve on the profits and entirely take care by lowering on the losses. This, in the long run, enhances rapid and constant rise in your capital contribution. If you to do this; however, it will require that you be keen to observe the positions of your trade each day as longs they are open. You also need to adjust stop orders depending on the day's prices. In addition, you have to pick your profits or returns, based on the predefined plans all the time you reach your targets.

There are master plan rules that aid in the control of open positions daily and can help in their closure at the rightful times, starting with those which constantly reduces the chances of loss suffering. The phenomenon is referred to as trailing stop loss.

As soon as your trade is kicked off and the opening price determined, the first item onboard is to establish your stop loss level, thus join the correlating order. What next will come by the following day at the opening of the next days? This is the time as you initialize your trade; you need to observe the opening behavior of your very stock closely. Whenever it opens with a price that closes to the last day's close so to say, it gaps up not or down, you to need to tune up your stop-loss level depending on the previous days prices nonetheless, when it gaps upwards or even downwards by saying 50 cents or greater for every share, then you will be required to shift the stop-loss level depending on the existing day's prices.

How to Improve On Your Profit Projections

Master plan has rules developed to improve your profit expectations. As you initiate an order with a projected target of the profit, you only apply it to 0.50 of the shares you bought. Whenever you reach your target and hence execute the closing order, thus locking in an increase of 7% on the part of your stock say half, then you retain the other part of your share to gain from any future increase in price.

The agenda, in this case, is to ride the full wave for the limited time remaining, thus taking advantage of all the profit. At this point in time, instead of allowing all your profit to ride on that order, you will have to place atop order so as to exit or get out all of the remaining position.

Chapter 6: Risk Management

What's A Risk or Risks in Swing Trade?

To begin with, first of all, we need to understand the meaning of risk and appreciate the effect they have on trading. To risk is simply to prepare and be ready for the outcome of inevitable. Is a science or even art as it may deem proper depending on the user, associated with loss limiting that may affect your portfolio. It can be divided into two levels. Management of risks at individual security or portfolio level. This can be accomplished in the following manner:

a)   Regulate the capital investment to your position, thus sizing of your position

b)   Identify the securities that are more liquid to invest in.

c)   Take advantage of several positions where you should spread your capital across.

d)   Widen the scope of your capital investment

e)   Measure the level of the risk in stocks before you get in for them. By so doing, you will be securing your portfolio.

Using the unknown to work out the known. In business, there are many puzzles to fill. There are many unknown constants there are known ones. So in general someone beginning a business or venturing into a given business plan, we can say he is risking his resources for the unknown hoped-for or profits.

Options pose as a potential area of investment where many investors are so much willing to invest in. Will the options being one of the most flexible yet profit-making ventures, traders are supposed to have the knowledge of the merits and demerits of the same business before they join. And as well they also need to have some prior knowledge of the challenges the venture poses for this, in the long run, will be able to assist them whenever it comes to decision making.

Considering all the strategies of options, we should be informed of the potential setbacks as well as the benefits we expect as we join the trade. We must also be ready to take up the losses if they happen to come. All successful and perhaps experienced traders, who have been in the business for quite long   will want to agree with me that, risk management is a concept which everyone   else   has   to   take   in   for   long   term profitability, and most specifically lowering the potential losses for every trade to a given level in time of any given account. If you interview some traders, you will find out that there is a common figure that is ever reiterated, i.e., 5%, implying that most trades cost the 5% of your general ledger or account. Figures that are greater than that ever increases the negative feeling that will interfere with your judgment in the long run.

Your activity may, therefore, assume a character that is more of gambling than anything else. Therefore you need to manage the risks carefully by limiting potential losses from every trade to about 5% of your account.

Assumptions and Imaginations.

Assumptions and imaginations basically lead to misconceptions. Nothing actually should be left to imagination or assumption as long as you are in the business. There is this phenomenon of thinking that you are the mafia who knows how to handle challenges as they arise, but also you could result into a potential loser for the market has its own trends, or rules defined to govern it. Whenever you put together a series of your winnings in trades, you may end up developing some great confidence in the skills and strategies that you are using as a swing trader. That could be good for you.

However, if your confidence, on the contrary, is displaced by arrogance, then, be sure of the notion that you may encounter enough risks in your business. Regardless of your current position in business, remember there are other business people out there who are well informed and have higher knowledge and skill and even well prepared than you. All humble traders do admit mistakes as they come or arise as opposed to all arrogant traders who believe that it's the market that perhaps is posing a great challenge to them and not their own mistake. They think they are right.

There is a misconception that every day is Friday or the notion that all swans are white. The fact that you enjoyed profits on Friday doesn't mean that you sit back and relax, thinking that markets will bring about profits as you achieved on Friday. Or simply have no knowledge of the existence of other types or colors of swans does not mean that in reality, they do not exist. Knowledge can be viewed as the ability to understand someone's ignorance. Financial markets are ever teaching this kind of lesson to millions each day. Sometimes you may think that you really know more than you actually do. A big lie.

One of the most misleading phenomena is the idea of drawing conclusions based on a single event. In the event of trading, you cannot presume that some aspects may not occur simply because you have never encountered them before. Similarly, you can't just believe that since some events have occurred before now, they will continue occurring that way.

You can plan to manage your risks well if you anticipate negativity even though they may never come to existence than if you are just optimistic thus no room for inevitable.

You Need Education

One of the areas that pose as a risk factor is the area of education to traders. Most traders if not all, believe that by knowing or having the knowledge of trading tools, then, you are good to go. How wrong they are. A market as we may term it is a living organism. You are supposed to watch carefully on the trends, and whatever surrounds them, you also need to read enough literature of whatever markets or rather businesses entail.

You need to set and goals of at least equipping yourself with the business knowledge of the markets and the trading concept by reading at least a book after a certain period of time say a month or so. If you keep up with the spirit of acquiring new information, then you will limit the fact that you are know-it-all, and therefore when it comes to business trading, you can comfortably challenge the fate of the so-called " smart-traders", who poses with a smart 'IQ', yet not smart in real practice.

These imposters pose so impressing profits for a limited period only to find themselves out of the trade since they do not have the capacity beat up or cope up with the risks that the swing trade has or even admit that they made mistakes.

There Must Be Concentration And Technical Analysis.

You need to have some knowledge of the technicalities of the stocks and as well as commodities. As a swing trader, the analysis should be done from a technical viewpoint. Various risks come up as a result of lack of Concentration. Most prominent business people ever concentrate on single businesses. Whenever you lay your time and resources in a given venture or business, it is easy to monitor the trends as the market changes, reductions in values of stocks, high-risk factors affecting the businesses such increased taxes or superimposed taxes, therefore, we can say that you have full control over the business. We can relate this to a taxi driver who is partly driving and surfing the internet or responding to a short message service while driving. In this case, it is easy and quite inevitable that the taxi driver may end up causing a fatal accident due to lack of Concentration or divided attention. In the same way, a trader who does not put more attention to a single business may end up losing it to others after realizing great loses.

He can quit the trade even though it does not exhibit any critical challenges that yield quitting.

Shock Resistance (Develop Shock Absorbers):

In swing trading, you need to have what we call shock resistance. This is an attribute of only strong traders. It is not good to quit the business after the first challenge, say encountering a loss. You need to understand that a business is a growing concern. This means that the more you are in the business venture, the more you are knowledgeable and experienced and therefore, the greater the chances of maneuvering within the same business.

There are loses and profits that you will be making as you continue with the business. Loses should teach you the action for the next course, whereas profit should encourage or motivate you to increase- on the level of investment capital. None of the above should make you quit the trading game. All other factor kept constant; a trader must be strong and confident.

You need to be resistant to pressure. There is completion in every market and more especially when the stocks are moving at a fairly competitive price.

If you have sit and wait, it isn't waiting for you

You do not need to appreciate so much the credentials that you own; you need to work with your intrinsic. Best ever trades just emerge as a surprise and will always be grabbed by those ready. They may be urgent. You need to turn around almost instantly to get hold of the opportunity before it escapes.

Proper Timing

Ensure that whatever you do has to be time-bound. Even the movement in the prices is determined by time cycles. If you trade in proper time cycles, you are assured of success in your business. If you become a good time watchman, you will be able to avoid many setbacks and limiting the risk of failure.

You need to understand that even the prices are conscious. They may repeat themselves at whatever specific interval. Only you need to be conscious of the timings in order to enjoy on that advantage.

Be a Great "Riskier"

Many people run to where everyone else is running to. As it has been anciently said, that rivers follow routes that have the least resistance so are the many who would want to venture into these businesses. Least do you know that where there is much competition, the gain is very minimal? Find a set up that is so scary because that exactly is the one you need to trade-in. You should never expect it to be so attractive until you make your profits out of it. If it gave you good returns, then it is evident that every Tommy and Jerry would trade it. Whatever begins with flowers at the end will give thorns. As anciently said that not all that glitters is gold. Whatever at first brings pain literally ends up in wonderful pleasure.

Always Be Outstanding In Your Operations

Always trade in a contrary manner to the crowds. Either ahead or behind but not on the same level. Do not go with excitements. You need to be the pacesetter being able to walk in profits and the first to move out of them. You should be very vigilant to get hold of their finances before they grab yours. You should find pride in other peoples' misfortunes. Take in and work out of others ill advises and achieve much during their mourning periods.

Contradict the Open

Join the business when they least expect and exit when they really need you. Never give room for your competitors to understand your tricks lest they work out your demise.

Big moves are hidden at the back of the extremes with a trading range. Do not be moved by the masses for your entry alert. Masses can attract you, and by the time you opt-in, it may be too late for you. This may result in painful losses on your part as others are enjoying the profits of the trade.

Take Care Of Inevitable As You Seek For Rewards

You need to be every vigilant by putting on market chastity. You will be considered immature if your attention always revolves around profits; however, Concentration on loss management is a clear indication of experience. As we all know, markets have no single intention of dissipating funds to those who won't earn it. So you need to be so keen about that. Do not concentrate so much on getting back your money; it will definitely come to pass, concentrate on the game and the gimmicks.

Losses Pose Warnings Before They Occur

Whenever you get a loss, no one should carry your cross other than yourself. Perhaps there were indicators to the same, but you decided to hold on based on assumptions. If you move in this trend, you may absorb a lot of pain of losing before you admit the fact.

Indiscipline the Key to Failure

You may have all the necessary knowledge concerning the trade, but you lack discipline. Your failure is at hand. It has been said once and again that discipline is the key to success. This is very true. Discipline is the driving force and power towards the achievement of great and smart returns not just returns. Listen to your inner man. It could be a small voice speaking to you softly, yet it is the determinant of your winning. Recall: In most cases, the most successful part of your trading won't be entertaining at all; instead, it will be so boring just as it is for the hustle you are having right now.

The greatest determinant for becoming a successful swing trader lies in the fact that you can execute your own individual concept of risk management. The whole concept lies in putting all eggs in one basket. You should be able to diversify the holdings and put a limitation on the investment in only one security. Even though diversification poses to be a great player in managing risks, it does not entail all necessary features of the same. As well traders never plan their diversification well, therefore, losing it all at the end of the day.

Risk management can be categorical in nature. It can be summarized in three areas.

i.   Lower the risk from arising from just one commonplace.
ii.   Consider limiting the risk on the levels of your portfolio
iii.   And effecting the orders as from your risk system. You can be your own worst enemy in swing trading. The market could result in punishing you.

Trading basically can be so complicated. It is not always the way you perceive a thing is what they are.

Chapter 7: Factors Affecting Options Prices

Before getting into options trading, you should first understand the factors that influence options prices. Options prices are not limited to the cost of the underlying stock. As a trader, you can never tell the price of an option until you understand the elements that contribute to its value. The process of putting a price tag to an option involves a lot of complex techniques, processes, and strategies. Every option value that you come across as not just a random figure. It represents a series of calculations and derivatives that are calculated using a number of financial models. One such model is the Black Scholes Model, which we discuss next.

Intrinsic and Time Value of Options

The price of an option is also known as the premium. This is the price per share of the underlying stock. An option's premium can be viewed in two dimensions. There is time value and intrinsic value. Generally, the time value and intrinsic value are added together to come up with the premium. But this is only a basic figure since there are several other factors that also play an important role in determining the final price of an option.

By definition, the intrinsic value of an option is the value it would have if it were exercised on that very day. In other terms, it is the price at which the strike price is – in-the-money or the value of an option that has not been lost to time decay. An option is in the money when it has some profits in it for the buyer. For instance, a call option worth $30 on a stock that's trading at $40 is $10 in the money. If the buyer decides to exercise the call option at this point, there will be a profit of $10. Options that are out of the money always have an intrinsic value of zero since there is no profit realized by the buyer in such a scenario.

The time value of an option is the additional amount that an investor can pay to realize more profit before the option contract expires. For instance, if an option is scheduled to expire in a month's time, there is a possibility for the time value to go high since there is more opportunity for the option to rise or decline in value over the weeks. If an option is expiring today, there will be little change in the time value because there is no room for the option to change in value.

Time value is, therefore, the difference between an options premium and the intrinsic value. When it comes to deriving the price of options, these two values matter a lot because they determine the profit investors can get should they decide to purchase a certain option. The intrinsic value determines the value of the option at that particular time, while the time value helps predict the future value of an option. These two values also help in establishing the risks involved in a particular trade.

The Black Scholes Model and Pricing of Options

The most important thing in options trading is profit. In basic financial trading, the profit is derived from getting the difference between purchase costs and payoff prices. This is not the case with options and models such as the Black Scholes model provides an easy way to determine your supposed profits.

This model is simply a formula or equation used by traders to value their investments. The model works by generating the value of an option in relation to the contract prices. It combines several variables such as the cost of the underlying stock, expiration date, the volatility of the stock, and the interest rates to come up with an estimated cost for the options. Before using this model to price your options, you must note that it works on a number of assumptions that may affect the outcome of your calculations. Here are some of them.

1.   The model assumes that no dividends are earned from the underlying stock

2.   The current market and interest rates will not change during the entire trading period

3.   It works best with European options since it assumes that you can only exercise at expiration

4.   No dividends will be paid on the underlying stock during the entire trading period

5.   It does not factor transaction costs in buying an option

6.   Volatility is constant

7.   Options returns are distributed in equal spreads

Despite these assumptions, the model is very helpful when it comes to options pricing, and most traders who are uncertain of their figures use it to predict trading scenarios and identify the cost of options.

The Black Scholes pricing model had stood the test of time since 1973 when it was developed. It was the first options pricing formula on the market and was used extensively to derive the theoretical price of most options.

To date, traders and options investors depend on it to price their calls and puts. The model utilizes a geometric Brownian motion formula that records volatility and drifts in prices. It is, therefore, capable of capturing the constant changes in time value, expiration dates, and other factors.

Black Scholes Model Formula

The model's formula is quite complicated. The good thing is that you do not need to understand how mathematics works since you can use online or offline calculators to get the figures. Some trading platforms have in-built calculators too that can help you get the prices in no time. The call option formula is obtained through multiplying the stock value with the normal probability distribution function. The strike price is then multiplied by the normal distribution and the resultant value subtracted from the first calculation. This is summarized in the formula below.

$$\text{Theoretical option price} = pN(d_1) - se^{-rt}N(d_2)$$

$$\text{where } d_1 = \frac{\ln\left(\frac{p}{s}\right) + \left(r + \frac{v^2}{2}\right)t}{v\sqrt{t}}$$

$$d_2 = d_1 - v\sqrt{t}$$

The variables are:

p - stock price

s - striking price

t - time remaining until expiration, expressed as a percent of a year

r - current risk-free interest rate

v - volatility measured by annual standard deviation

ln - natural logarithm

N(x) - cumulative normal density function

From the above formula, it is clear that the model utilizes six variables to derive the price of an option. These are:

1. The type of option (call or put)
2. The time available before the option expires
3. The strike price
4. Price of the underlying stock
5. Stock volatility Interest rate

Why you need to Understand This Model

Before thinking about using the formula above in your calculations, it is necessary to understand the role it plays in the options market. Here are a few things that may be of help to you.

1. The formula indicates that the time left before an option expires directly affects the price of a put or call option. It assumes that the more time there is to trade the option, the higher the price.
2. It also indicates that a stock's volatility also determines the price of an option. Volatility refers to the range through which the stock price changes in each day. The higher the volatility, the higher the changes in the value of the option.
3. The model makes you believe that rumors and earning releases can make option prices to change significantly. A positive rumor will impact the price

positively, while a negative rumor causes the price to decline.

Major Factors Influencing Pricing

1. Cost of the Underlying Stock

Options are derivatives of underlying securities. When a call option is in-the-money, you can exercise it at a profit because it has gained intrinsic value. A put option is said to be in-the-money when the stock price is less than the strike price. These changes in stock prices do define the closing price of an option. Any time you purchase a call option, and the underlying stock increases in value, the cost of the option increases. If the stock prices decline, then the option's value will decline as well. The pricing of stocks is normally affected by factors such as demand and supply as well as other fundamental and technical factors relating to trading chart patterns and the market's momentum.

2. The Strike Price

Options strikes are also categorized as in-the-money and out-of-the-money. A call option is in the money when the stock price is above the strike price. The opposite is true when the call is out-of-the-money. Options which are in-the-money return higher value than those that are out-of-the-money. As for puts, the lower the strike price, the greater the input and premium. Therefore the cost of an option will be greatly affected by the strike price.

3. **Expiration Time**

Options have a time limit. The value of each option is greatly affected by how much time is available before the option expires. As the time of expiration nears, the price of the option becomes smaller and rapidly goes down until the last days of the option's existence. When there is a lot of time before expiration, an option has enough time to change course, but when the closing line is near, it is impossible for the option to change much. A considerable amount of time allows the underlying stock to make a significant movement. Once an option reaches expiration when it's out of the money, the contract expires worthless, and the trader makes no money from it.

Time has a great impact on the cost of options. In most cases, long trading periods work in favor of the trader since the charts can change significantly before the expiration date is reached. Since the value of an option decreases as the end date approaches, you must not wait for expiration to close positions.

4. **Type of Option**

Basically, options are of two types – call or put. The value of an option is often determined by its type. A call option allows you to purchase the underlying stock at a specified cost and time period while a put option allows you to sell the underlying asset, also at specified costs and time period. Buying calls and selling puts increases the value of your option. Buying puts and selling calls cause the value of your options to decrease.

5. **Interest Rates**

These have very little effect on the price of an option. When interests go high, the value of a call option goes high, and the value of a put option goes down. The theory behind this, states that if you purchase an option instead of stock, there is an amount of cash that you can save for interest purposes. The more the cash saved, the more the interests.

6. **Dividends**

Although options do not earn you dividends, their values tend to change whenever dividends of the underlying stock are released. When companies distribute dividends, they work using the ex-dividend date, and if you happen to own the underlying stock on the day of release, you will receive the dividends. As the amount of dividends increase, the value of the put option also increases, but the value of the call option decreases. Dividends do not affect the options directly. They affect the underlying stock. In most cases, the market falls whenever dividends are released.

7. **Volatility**

This is one of the most popular elements that affect prices in the options market. In simple terms, volatility refers to the rate at which price options change, either in a positive or negative way. High volatility often results in high prices, while low volatility causes low prices.

Volatility is in two types - historical volatility and implied volatility. Historical volatility refers to the predictable changes in the pricing based on past patterns. It is believed that future trends in the price of an option can be determined by previous performance. Implied volatility, on the other hand, utilizes historical data as well as current prices to determine an option's future value. The current price is derived from two closest out-of-the-money strike prices. This type of volatility is more dependable than the first one because it puts current market activity in consideration when determining the price of an option. It is written as a percentage, and one of its characteristics is that it is non-directional. It is, therefore, upon the trader to determine whether the volatility will occur on the upside or downside of the strike price.

Volatility is only an estimate and not a calculated figure. In most cases, the higher the volatility, the more likely it is for the stock prices to change. These high stock prices automatically translate to high returns.

Volatility and the Option Skew

The option skew is another dimension to product pricing. It is common in volatile trades and works in relation to expiration dates and strike prices. In this concept, it is believed that options will bear different expiration dates and strike prices based on the value of the implied volatilities. This means that high volatility is to be expected more at some strike prices and expiration dates more than others.

The above factors are the most basic. There are several other more advanced factors that affect the value of an option indirectly by affecting the value of the underlying security. These can be categorized as fundamental factors and technical factors.

Fundamental Factors

These refer to a combination of the option's earning base and a valuation multiple such as the premium/ earnings ratio. As the stock owner, you have a claim on the profits realized from the stock. This is referred to as the earnings ratio. The earning base and valuation multiple affect the price of the underlying security. This, in turn, impacts the cost of an option.

The earning base is dependent on the type of company selling the stock shares. The valuation multiple is an expression of future expectations and is based on discounts applied to the present cost of the stock. Two factors affect the valuation multiple, that is the expected growth of the earning base and the potential discount rate. High growth rates translate to increased stock prices and increased call option values. High discount rates lower the stock price, thus lowering options values in case of a call. In most cases, the discount rate is a derivative of the perceived risk. Risky stocks often have higher discounts. Another factor that determines the discount is inflation. High inflation causes high discounts and low stock prices. Low inflation translates to low discounts and high options prices.

In summary, fundamental factors that affect the pricing of options are:

1. The underlying stock's earnings base
2. The expected growth of the base
3. Discount rates
4. Level of risk associated with the underlying stock.

Technical Factors

These comprise of a set of external conditions that affect the supply and demand of underlying securities in options trading.

They include:

Inflation

From a technical perspective, inflation is a great determinant of stock prices. Low inflation drives high stock prices, and high inflation drives low prices.

Market Strength and Sentiments

The value of options is also affected by the overall market trends as well as the psychology of other traders. For instance, you may use other factors to estimate the price of your options, but the market may repeat the same news over and over keeping the underlying security either artificially low or high. These market sentiments contribute to what is known as behavioral finance. The assumption always states that in most instances, markets are always unstable, and the instability is often caused by psychological and social factors.

The ideas that arise from behavioral finance are mostly suspicions and rumors. This is because traders tend to overemphasize some trends and data aspects that come to their mind, without studying the reality on the ground.

Substitute Financial Instruments

Sometimes, companies may compete for stock and options investment profits with other financial instruments on the global market. This may include things like commodities, bonds, equities, and real estate. This introduces multiple types of underlying securities, and since some of these instruments are not popular, their prices tend to change slowly, resulting in less or no changes in the cost of options. Illiquid financial tools are the most dangerous. Most investors avoid them because they are not popular on the market. Trading in such instruments will always result in decreased options prices.

Trends

Sometimes, the price of an option may simply change according to certain short-term trends. An options contract may gather an upward momentum causing significant increments in the price. Alternatively, the stock price may gain momentum in the reverse direction, causing a steep decline in the price of an option. One unfortunate attribute about trends is that they cut both ways, and therefore, the outcome is not always positive.

Options Pricing and News

Although it is impossible to measure the impact of financial news on the price of options, there are some developments that always impact investor sentiments. Political situations, product breakthroughs, mergers, and other unforeseen activities can have either a negative or positive impact on the value of an option's underlying security. Since most trading happens on global grounds, financial news can really impact investment in one way or another, and the impact is always immediate.

Pricing American versus European Options

American options are exercised any time during the trading process as long as the expiration date has not reached. European options can only be exercised on the expiration date. Exercising early adds value to options. This is why American options are considered more valuable than European options, although exercising the options early makes the contract sub-optimal.

Exercising options early can be of advantage to the pricing of options in several ways. For instance, whenever a company pays large dividends on the underlying stock, the value of the stock reduces significantly. Exercising an option derived from such stock just before the dividends are paid off can save you some profit in case of an in-the-money option. It can also save part of your premiums in the case of an out-of-the-money market. You may also need to exercise your put options when the underlying asset's value is deep-in-the-money so as to make maximum profits. You will only get some interest when the stock price is less than the put option's strike price.

Different traders use different factors to calculate the price of options. Short-term investors tend to consider technical factors over other metrics because these cause sudden changes in the value of the underlying security. Long-term options traders always consider a wide array of factors, especially those that affect the stock prices in the long run. Since traditional finance concepts do not seem to capture every aspect that affects the pricing of stocks, several exciting developments have come up around behavioral finance that is believed also to impact the price of options. The complexity of pricing options lies in the variables as well as the formulas involved in calculating the prices. With a good pricing model, however, you do not need to worry about leaving any of the factors mentioned above out when pricing your options. With these models, you only input the necessary variables and receive an answer that represents your option's worth.

Chapter 8: Swing Trading

This is a phenomenon that is characterized by frequent fluctuation in the stock prices and the market indices.

This kind of fluctuation is never constant as we can imagine but instead is wavy springing forth and backward, to and from thus creating a graph that can be analyzed with short swings across a fairly narrow range with a primary long term uptrend or downtrend. Many people who engage in this kind of trade do recognize it and thus appreciate it.

Definition

This is simply an investment strategy put in place to monitor and make profits from the frequent unstable or irregular short term wavy movements that occur in any well-formed market trend. The concept here is to identify the range and the trend of the market for you to gain profits or reduce losses that happen in the specified ranges.

Swing trading is a flexible technique, can be used with equal success in both up and down markets. Therefore if a specific trading range can be established, then the concept can be profitable for the businesses that are moving sideways.

The swing trading analogy is a more of opportunistic than realistic because the trader makes an effort to watch or view the trends and therefore will always concentrate so much in the direction of movement of the markets and hence the adage "the trend is your friend."

There are three basic categories in which we can analyze the swing trader's strategic options, namely: bullish, bearish, and range bound.

Range-Bound

Whenever you hear someone talk of stock being range-bound, this simply indicates that the market prices are locked in the sideways pattern. That's to say that swing trader will either by on short term pullbacks to the long term support level or even sell the products on short term rallies to the long term resistance level.

Bearish

When we talk about the stocks primary trend is bearish, it implies that it is moving downwards. What the swing trader, in this case, do I to watch for the rally to the long term resistance level and sell thus shares short, as he looks for a near-term pullback to the stocks most recent previous.

Bullish

Lastly, this trend signifies the upward movement of the stocks. In this case, the trader will look the pullback to the long-term support level and then buy shares, thus playing for a short-term rebound to the stock's most recent previous high.

These are the basic primary indicators that can be used to establish the best swing trading opportunities as well as precise guidelines as regards to the entry or exit points and how to well allocate one's assets to any given market at any given time I business. As you may be knowing, in business, there are long term investors or traders as well as day to day traders. There are a set of similarities and differences in every category of trading paradigm. We shall be able to consider just but a few.

Bearing in mind that any trader in the market, whether, long term, swing or short –term or day to day trader, the primary objective is to make a profit out of the same business.

1. **Long Term Investor**

This can also be referred to as a long-term trader. This is simply defined as a buy and hold phenomena. This type of investment calls for a lengthy period of time over which a sale of shares is made or made. He buys shares, holds them for a good period say a year or so before he releases the shares for trade on the market. In this type of style, the trader only initiates the sale of his shares about three to five times a year. He depends entirely on the nature of growth in the stocks, which determines his buying and selling decisions. He will always want to invest in a large-per share risk, giving his stock ample time to change in price as he waits for the expected enormous shift to kick in. As a result of a limited number of trades done in a period of time; therefore, the total dollar value of the trader's market activity is quite small. Hence the total transaction costs are as well limited as compared to the day today or even the swing trader. A 23 to 30 percent annual return, in this case, is a very highly acceptable level of performance for this type of trader with 50 percent being considered as relatively outstanding.

2. **Day Traders**

As the name suggests, this is a trader who does business on a daily basis. He can make even up to a satisfactory number of sales per day depending on the level of investment in the business; thus, the stock he has on the market. It could be 2 to 5- five or even more rounds of shares traded in a day. He has nothing much to consider other than the ever-fluctuating prices or the shifting trends in the prices of the shares every hour of the day.

What worries him most is the number of transactions he can be able to handle or do in a day as long as the trading period or time of day that's the close of the business time of the specific day. The day trader is not conscious of the company's long term prospects because he is not looking for major profits rather a25 cents per share or even less is satisfactory to his objectives. He is not challenged by the slight shift in the share price dropdown for will always capitalize on the next upward shift in the price and therefore realize his profit however small it could be to help curb the previous negative skew on the shares. This indicates that as a day trader, one has to have sufficient working capital to put into the business in order to take advantage of the vast business and hence make much out of the day as he keeps watch on content shifting trends. He needs to have a very strong heart and not easily give up spirit because of the nature of the fluctuating trends in the market value of the shares at every ever-changing minute or an hour and the high commission charges.

It is of great importance that we as well need to know the importance of these two types of traders which we have talked about briefly. You may have tried the swing trading and as a result, would like to adventure in the possible alternative type of trade. As we all know, in this case, the swing trader is a concoction of these two types of trades we have just discussed in brief above. We can refer to it as 'hybrid trade,' as it has features of both day to day and long term investing.

Characteristics of Swing Trading

As we have seen before, the day to day trader makes his sales on a daily basis as opposed to the long term trader or investor. The relationship, in this case, is the fact that the swing trader ranges in the middle of the two styles of trading.

- He is a goal rather than a time-bound. His driving force is his goal or whatever objective he has in the trade rather than time. He does not have any well defined time to exit his positions rather will always hold on until the price objective is met. The time, however, may not be so long for it could just be five to ten days or even a month.

- Swing trader depends entirely on his technical analysis for his entry or even exit signals. He joins the trade when the stocks pull back to support level as fluctuates within the primary bullish trend, or else moves high a resistance level while shifting in a primary bearish trend.

- The profit objectives are set depending on the width of the stock's recent trading channel within its major trend, and can always range somewhere from $1.50 to $3.0 per share, depending on the initial price of the stock.

- The swing trader needs to pay more attention to fundamentals than the day trader. This is to avoid other negative reports during the expected holding period.

- The swing trader follows a great number of stocks say 20 to 25 issues and must be well invested, thus grabbing every new opportunity as soon as the former one is closed. Therefore a swing trader may make a trade or even two every day. As opposed to the day trader, he can skip a day or two minus trading as long as he is fully invested or if no opportunities come up.

- As for the swing trader, his portfolio is overturned regularly. Therefore, his capital requirement is lower than the long term investor; hence, his commission burden higher, though it's still far lower compared to the day to a day trader. It has a clear cut entry and exit criteria, which is less demanding as compared to the two other trading platforms. Therefore it is easy t build a strong record of successful trades making average annual returns of about 55, 100, or even up to 200.

Chapter 9: Swing Trading With Call Option

To start off, we need firs to remind ourselves what an option is. We can refer an option to as a contract which accords its owner the right and not the obligation to choose between buying or selling part of the underlying assets at an already known price either before or at the expiry of the contract.

Options enhance one's portfolio. This is by use of added income, leverage, and protection. Options as well are types of derivatives' security. This is, so reason being that their prices are connected to the prices of other items.

When you understand the terminologies applied or used and the relevant rules for the options are very imperative for one to begin trading in them.

Options can be used applied in a wide scope of strategies from the most shallow to the very high-risk ones hence offer to attract a multitude of investors at first.

What's A Call?

A call is a right. Call option, therefore, is a right given to the very owner to purchase a stock. It could be termed as a down payment for a certain purpose in the future.

Example:

Suppose we have a 'potential' prospective property owner call it real estate. He could see emerging developmental changes around the estate. Probably he may wish to have the right to purchase the real estate but in the future. He would only wish to exercise that right as soon as the major improvements are effected near the scene done to his satisfaction. He could either profit in the option of acquiring it or else not.

He has the choice of buying the call option from the estate owner or the person developing it in order to buy it at a price say $500,000 at whatever interval in time, and it could be after a period of even five years. This is a deposit which does not call for a refund. In a real sense, the owner or the person developing the estate could be able to grant that option free of charge. Thus the incumbent buyer of the property must provide something like a down payment in order to restrain the property to him.

As far as the option is concerned, we refer this cost to as a premium. Simply meaning 'cost of an option contract.' In our case above, the amount could say $30,000, which the prospective buyer gives to the seller or the developer whatsoever. We could imagine that a period has gone two years down the line and the place has been improved drastically even zoning done or approved then the buyer of the very estate exercises the option r light away and buys the estate at the agreed price being the purchased contract.

Relatively the value of the property at that time might have doubled to $1000, 000, yet the already give down payment locked the price of the estate, the buyer will only pay the $500,000. Suppose the zoning approval doesn't take effect until the elapse of the stipulated time, in this case, the buyer is forced to pay for the asset according to the existing market price for the contract will have expired. In either way, the owner of the property does not give back the $30,000 that was given him to lock in the option.

Buying and Selling Calls

Whenever you buy a stock, it will give you a long position. Similarly, a call option when bought gives you a prospective long position in the fundamental stock.

When you short sell a stock, you get a short position; therefore, selling a 'naked,' call will yield a fundamental short position in the principal stock.

Long Call

We have long call as short call options. In regard to the long call option, you can only apply it if you have projections of an upward trend of the market in a bullish way. Whenever this happens, you will have the right to exercise the options; allow the expiry of the options as well you can resell the option. If you allow your option to expire, it means that you stand a high risk of losing your investment in the same call purchase. You could rather exercise the very option. You will be required to have the necessary capital to purchase the stock. And suppose you initiated a trade via purchasing a call option, you may be forced to sell it off in grab the profit.

Use of Long Call Strategy for Speculation

As you may be aware, most investors normally begin with the purchase of stock. They are therefore used in thinking that the prices of that stock will always go up before they dispose of it. Similarly, new option interested traders begin by the purchase of call options because it looks closely like what they are used to doing prior to this.

Whenever a call option on security is bought, ever referred to as 'going long,' the option, whoever the holder of the call is mandated to control the stock in its absence? I.e., he does not necessarily have to own it right away. He only does so for a certain stipulated amount of money. We term a long call as the leveraged option to the main stock. When the stock prices move up, the value of the option similarly goes up even very high but on percentage grounds. The leverage in question can yield a great percentage profit simply because buying of calls needs less for capital commitment as compared to an instant purchase of a stock.

The profits, in this case, are unlimited theoretically now that there is no any limitation over the increase in the stock price. There is yet another advantage of not losing anything greater than the value of your initial investment. You can lose the whole value of the premium even though you may not lose even a coin on the potential value you invested. We refer calls with fixed prices that are higher than .the existing stock price to as out of the money options. Suppose today was the expiration day, then it means that they would be rendered worthless.

Out of the money, options can only hold water as long as the expiration dates have not yet been reached, therefore there is still more room for the stock prices to go up beyond their strike prices. Time premium is, therefore, that part of the option assigned to time. When an options strike price is equivalent to the stock price, we refer to that as at the money call option. The premium that is paid up for 'at the money,' option is also governed by time. It may not take much of an up in the price of the stock before turning the same into an in the money option.

In the money call, the option's strike price is less than the existing stock price. The intrinsic value is the difference between the current stock price and the strike price. This is the amount that the option is in the money. Whenever there is some time left to the expiration date, the 'in the money,' option is capable of being split into two different parts namely:

- Intrinsic value
- Time value.

In summary, the further the 'out of the money,' option can be, the cheaper it could be thus the greater the leverage. If a stock makes a fast quick advance to your favor out of the money option may result in doing you a great job by increasing your money. However, if this process doesn't occur very fast, the out of the money options may work out to your disappointment. Therefore 'in the money and out of the money,' options do move closely as the underlying stock simply because they have a greater delta. At the money has got a delta that is around 0.5 implying that if the stock moves a point, then there is a significant move of a half a point for the option. In- the -money options their delta are close to one, for the move close of point to point in relation to stock. Many people have various reasons as to why they buy options. Some who do not have the exact amount required could opt to purchase options infractions of the cost. The fact that there are limited risks motivates many investors who would wish to lower their downside hence limit to the price of the option. There are those investors who just want to take the great advantage of the leverage that exists while speculating or working on the shifting of the prices.

Bull Call Spread

As we have said before, option trade beginners, do buy calls most. I wish they considered the benefit spreads have. A bull call spread is useful when you are hoping that the prices of a given stock may rise but still would ant little risk factor as opposed to a call purchase. It is a simultaneous process involving the purchase of a call option as well as selling another call option at a higher price but within the same month of expiration. The greatest advantage of this concept here is that it lowers the end product of the big enemies of long options being volatility an time. It is not very sensitive to the day today ups and downs portrayed in the stock prices and thereby being a more relaxed mode of trade expedition. One more benefit of the bull spread compared to the long call is that one is able to risk less capital for the same quantity of the contract. It lowers the break-even point as it heightens the chance s of profit-making.

Short Call

Likewise, calls can as well be sold for the sake of opening short call options. Basing on the forecast the stock's value may dwindle downwards, calls could be sold on that account. In this case, short calls make traders sell their stocks at   fixed prices in a specified time interval. Now that you are entrusting someone fully to purchase your stock, you will henceforth be provided with a premium for according them the right and an s such we refer this to as credit trade.

The premium given serves as the bid value for the option's real price. For the case of a directional trade, now that you believe regarding your prior analysis, a call can be traded off or sold on the fact there will be a reduction in its future value. Generally, short calls are directional trades. Whenever the stock's value goes higher compared to the strike price, of a call that you are required to sell that stock at a given strike price.

What Does The Short Call Obligate You To Do?

We refer assignment to an obligation to carry out an assignment. For the case of this scenario, you have the obligation of selling the stock. Similarly, another person in the near past bought the call and exercised his right and bought the stock at the fixed strike price, now that you also sold the call at a certain strike price, therefore are obligated to also sell the very stock at the stipulated strike price. Note: we refer a call to as being 'Naked' if it was sold without any combination with any other form of trade.

There are very strict requirements that brokerages have imposed on naked calls. For instance, 'account minimum,' of $100,000. It is done this ay because of the UN limitedness of the risk should the stock escalate or go beyond the strike price. For this reason, it's advisable to sell both calls and other trades. This is called a covered call.

Covered calls are a very proactive way of creating more cash flows in order or to increase the value of the portfolio. The reason for call selling is n to grab the premiums in a way that you allow the options to expire in a more worthless manner depending on prior analysis and prospection that stocks wouldn't go up above the strike prices in a given arrange of time.

Chapter 10: Swing Trading With Put Option

A put option is different from a call option. A call option is buying security, whereas a put option is all about selling off the security. In this case, therefore, a buyer of a security is given the right of selling it at a fixed price either on or before the date of expiry. The writer most often referred to as the seller of the security or a put, is hence obligated to buy the relevant stock at the fixed price when it is exercised. Americans in nature are very optimistic. They tend to think or even imagine that the following day could be somehow better than the current day, so is as with stock prices. In that case, call options tend to be highly favored in relation to others. This is attributed to the fact that whenever prices of stock go high, there is a greater chance of making most profits. For instance, in 1973, after the introduction of exchange-traded options, put options were never there. People embraced call options only. It was only after four years down the lane is when put options on trades were introduced. That was 'June 1977'. We will now concentrate on the put option in this part. We will look at various spreads in the put option such as long put and bear put spreads that will help us in working out on a predictable drop in value. We will also consider factors to give out more income by the sale of naked puts and also credit spreads.

Long Put Strategy

This is also called the downside betting. Whenever you purchase a put, you are accorded the right of selling one hundred shares of the stock. Just as a call option, a put option similarly is a contract which explains briefly the strike price that you do have a right of selling the stock at and the expiry date. The buyers of the put option have rights of selling their stocks at the fixed price, although they may not do so right away. In this very case, the put option seller has the obligation of purchasing a stock at the fixed price as long as the put is assigned.

 Many investors have it easy in understanding calls, although the put option has more strength, which is rare with calls. In this case, the timecan be spent in getting to know the puts, and perhaps how to apply them well is time well utilized. Many terminologies referring to options that are applied here could be the direct opposite based on where they are used most often. Input options, the in the money may mean a put of which the strike price is greater than the existing stock or the current stock price. Whereas the at the money holds thus explains an option that has the strike price and the stock price the same. Out of the money, on the contrary, has got its strike price a bit lower than the current price of the stock.

Not so different from the call option, out of the money 'put option's,' has a position with greater leverage and a higher risk in relation to an at the money or rather in the money. Earlier on, we saw that an option buyer could lose strictly the amount that was paid for the option and no other thing. As opposed to the call option, where the profit perspective was not limited by anything now that there was no limit on how the stock prices could move. In a put option, a limit is there because the stock's price will never move lower beyond zero. Even though that is the case, there is still more room for profit-making with most stocks.

Similar weights of leverage, big profit potentials, and limited risks, which makes the purchase of calls more attractive work on put option too. There is only one enemy that an option buyer has, and that's the time decay. This is because e as the days go by, options keep on losing their values.

Therefore a speculative buying of puts will tend to work well only if you are to work in a short time interval. The same way it is with call options, so it is with put options in that there are also a series of strike prices that vary in values and expiry dates. Now that options that have varying strikes and times behave uniquely to stock price movements, therefore a decision concerning the type of option to buy is relatively imperative with puts. You shouldn't be influenced in any way by the lower price, to decide on which option to go for.

Cheap options could be out of the money or thus to say lower than the stock price, hence buying them could result in a diminishing hope of your success compared to if you bought 'at or in the money option.' The remaining time to the date of expiry is a very crucial factor in decision making agenda. Time will always work in the opposite direction of the options buyers wish soon after the execution of the order. You need to judge well the period of time it may take for the stocks to shift in prices. Then multiply by two.

This, in turn, must help you find the expiration month to put in mind. Then you should strive to know the volatility situation at hand by constantly checking on the volatility chart. It will give you room to precisely know if generally as it has been said, options are expensive or cheaper for the stock in question. If the volatility implied is quite high, then consideration should be put on the purchase of in the money options only. Such options come with little time premiums, and as such, they are not very strict on the shifting of the volatility.

You could also wish to put into consecration the use of spreads to lower the volatility risk in this particular context. There is an immediate alternative to this worrying challenge, and that's the bear put spread. Much there are very many strengths than weaknesses of the put options, and it does not erase the fact that its limitations are also enormous to any business person.

Bear Put Spread

This is the speculative agenda to the downside with the spreads. With the use of bear put spreads, this is one way of playing a down market. The risks encountered on the purchase of an option compared to a vertical debit spread is just as correct in relation to putting as when you are using call. The ones with bearish price hopes could really buy a vertical debit spread that has put usually referred to as a bear put spread.

Therefore the bear put spread takes care of the maximum possible loss as well as the profits. Now so long as the most expected profit is greater than the possible loss, one could accept that the risk may carry some weight .i.e. not so steep. In bear put spread, it involves the purchase of a put option hence selling the same option that's located or situated further out of the money. One advantage that a put spread has is the fixing of maximum loss although it has got an offsetting demerit of fixing the highest profit.

The similar attribute of raised commissions yet slower development in the area of profit that is comparative to the purchase of an option relates to the bear put spread. Having all these in mind, not all may be interested, but as for the starters in the option investment, they are mostly very comfortable having the risk profile of the trade and on the other hand take in the limitations.

Selling Of Naked Puts

You can generate a lot of income in the sale of the naked puts. This is done by the direct sale of the option. In the beginning, it was mentioned that the sale of naked calls was a very risky exercise that wasn't so pleasing to the potential investors however with the selling goof naked puts does not show the similar type of risk. Basing on the short put strategy, out of the money or even at the money, puts are actually sold on the stocks which the trader doesn't mind owning.

Even though stocks are recurrent of the prices, or even increases, the very investors maintain the premiums even though the option expiry is worthless. One requirement of this strategy is margin; therefore, you need to invest much money in the brokerage account to take charge of the position suppose it is exercised. Else the strategy is also well-referred to as a "cash-secured" put. Assuming that there is a decline in the stock prices! one shouldn't worry so much, because as soon as it happens , the investor will immediately be assigned the shares and now the cost of the shares will be the strike price of the same put subtract the received premiums.

That is the factor to be considered because the writers are now required to purchase the stock and ensure they have enough cash left before joining the position.

For instance, suppose a stock is trading currently at $42.50, it means that the out of the money put that has a strike price of say 40 may be traded for as much as $2.50 giving out a credit to the account you own of or worth $25o. This is the amount that you own, and therefore you need to keep it however much whatever happens. Suppose you end up in a worse case, and you may be required to pay up to $4,000 for the 100 shares of the stock. If we remove the $250 and therefore the effective basis be $37,750, we can conclusively say Kudos! If you decide to go naked with say a put, your hope is that perhaps the stock price may go higher. This is a bullish position so it could be having the same expectations in the price as if you bought buy calls.

In this case, there is a difference in that, and call buyers are supposed to be keen to fight with the time decay. The prices for the stock s supposed to move high enough in order to take the cover of the time value as they generate a profit.

On the other hand, put sellers experience time decay so much. Therefore, they really embark on considering the time value to go downward. Even if the stock doesn't move at whatever level, the short put position will still be profitable. Now there is a great differentiating factor between a long call and a short put options in that it is quite hard to profit from the purchase of calls as it is very highly profitable to create profits from the sale of puts. It is very easy to make profits by the selling of puts, reason being the time value.

The downward change or movement it the time value, works greatly against the potential buyer; however, it is a valuable credit to the seller in the long run. Once someone goes naked on put, he is actually exposed to the high risk of making sure he should buy 100 shares of the stock at the strike price. Now, in this case, the owner of the put shall be allowed to exercise it only if it is "in the money."

This signifies that he would purchase the stocks at relatively higher the current price on the market. It sounds like a shocking outcome; however, you need to consider the strike price as a fair price for your stock. You expect a lot of inaccuracies on the market, and even some companies' stocks are ever undervalued. Suppose it happens that way, if you have 100 shares put in your ownership, you could still sound only if you will be willing to hold on the market. Whenever you sell a put, you get a premium that is credited to your very account. We call that income although it can discount the price of the entire stock suppose there is an exercise.

www.ingramcontent.com/pod-product-compliance
Lightning Source LLC
Chambersburg PA
CBHW070341220526

45467CB00001B/212